DON'T BE AFRAID HEAVEN IS REAL

"I SAW IT WITH MY OWN EYES AND FELT IT THROUGH MY ENTIRE BEING."

"AND THEY OVERCAME HIM BY THE BLOOD OF THE LAMB, AND BY THE WORD OF THEIR TESTIMONY; AND THEY LOVED NOT THEIR LIVES UNTO DEATH."
REVELATION 12:11

CHRISTOPHER SLAGER
"BIG C"

DO NOT BE AFRAID HEAVEN IS REAL
ISBN: 978-0-578-25498-2
Copyright © 2021 by Christopher Slager "Big C"
Published by Saving Our Generation Publishing

Saving Our Generation Ministries
P.O. Box 702624
Tulsa, Oklahoma 74170
SOGGlobal.org
ChrisBigCSlager.com

All scripture quotations in this book are from the *King James Version* of The Bible.

Printed in the United States of America

Dedication

I would like to dedicate this book to God the Father, God the Son, and God The Holy Spirit, the Holy Trinity. I dedicate this book to my mother, Rosie Slager, my father, Frank Slager, and all of my family. I dedicate this book to all of my mentors, pastors, and those who have supported me along the way. This book is dedicated to all of my friends and future friends. I dedicate this book to the body of Christ and the Kingdom of God. I dedicate this Book to every person who reads it, including you. I glorify and praise God for this book. This book is a God-given miracle.

"And Jesus looking upon them saith, with men it is impossible, but not with God: for with God all things are possible."
Mark 10:27

TABLE OF CONTENTS

INTRODUCTION

Heaven is real and I saw it with my very own eyes and felt it through my entire being. I never asked God to take me there but He did when I was eighteen years old. I was running away from Jesus and did not want to live for God. I was in a negative lifestyle, a sinful lifestyle that was going to eventually take me to prison or a cemetery at an early age. This divine encounter with me going to Heaven changed everything for me. A lot of people wonder what happens when they die. A lot of people are afraid of death. I believe after you read this book you will no longer be afraid of dying, and your eyes will open up to the truth just like mine were. For whatever reason God took me to Heaven and I believe it is because He wanted me to share about it with this world. We are simply passing through this earth. What God showed me was so glorious beyond words. Heaven is glorious, amazing, wonderful, and awesome. Heaven is a real place.

I am a living miracle of God, a living testimony of God's grace. I wrote this book to glorify God and to praise Him for who He is and for His everlasting mercy, grace, and love. My birth was a miracle, my childhood was a miracle, my teen life was a miracle, and my life in general is a miracle of God. How I surrendered my life to Jesus Christ is one big testimony and miraculous work of God. This book in itself is a miracle as I never thought I could write one. We serve a God of miracles. Your life is a miracle. You are a miracle.

I want you to know that your life is precious, and that you matter and are important to God. You have a God-given destiny and purpose for your life. The true living God, our Heavenly Father, is a God of forgiveness, love, and mercy. His arms are wide open and ready to receive you. He is ready to embrace you and He loves you tremendously. Enjoy this God-given piece of literature knowing that your life is going to be eternally impacted as you read it. I believe in you, I love you, and know that God is going to use your life as an instrument of His Grace. To God be all of the honor, glory, and praise in Jesus' name, amen.

In this Book I have included some of the greatest revelations that God's Holy Spirit has revealed to me in His Word that have made me the man who I am today in Christ Jesus. I believe that this book is going to be a major blessing to you. May it encourage and empower you to be who God has created you to be.

CHAPTER 1
THE HAND OF GOD

It all started in 1988 in a town called Hyannis in the beautiful State of Massachusetts. The third month of my mom's pregnancy she started bleeding in the womb, and the doctor said that I most likely was not going to make it. My mother and father are both people of faith. They called a prayer meeting with their Pastors at the time to believe for a miracle in the name of Jesus

Christ. Their pastors and friends fasted and prayed for my mother's healing at the name of Jesus. Everybody was in agreement for the healing miracle to take place. To put it in simple words the miracle happened, the bleeding stopped, and everybody praised God for the miracle. At the time my mom didn't know if she was going to have a girl or a boy. Their pastor said he heard from God that my mother would give birth to a son. He said, "this boy is going to preach, teach, and demonstrate the glorious Gospel of Jesus Christ to his generation." He said, "this boy is going to be used by God to bring eternal impact to the Nations of the world through the Gospel of Jesus Christ."

Six months went by and the pastor was correct on what he heard from God. Christopher Taques Slager, a baby boy, was born in Hyannis Hospital in the State of Massachusetts. The doctors did some routine tests on me that are done on newborn babies. After doing the tests, the doctor walked into my mother's hospital room with negative news. They found out that I was having blood issues and told her they were going to have to perform a blood transfusion that would be very risky, which required them to life-flight me in a helicopter to Boston Hospital so they could perform the blood transfusion there. My life was on the line and we needed another miracle from God.

Instead of panicking my mom and dad decided to stay shifted in faith. They put their trust in God and prayed over me in the name of Jesus, believing for another miracle. My dad got into his car and took off to the hospital in Boston as I was transported by the helicopter. The hospital in Boston was about one hour and thirty minutes by vehicle from where they were at. The doctor in Boston then notified the doctor in

Hyannis that the blood transfusion took place and was successful. My parents were updated on this and informed that I was going to be okay. God did it again, He again showed Himself faithful as another miracle took place for His glory. They immediately started praising God and celebrating Him for what He had done. They told all of their friends and family the good news and praised and glorified God together for the miracle.

THE UPBRINGING

    I was raised in Hyannis, Massachusetts until about the age of seven years old. When I was four, my parents decided to move out of the place where they were living into another apartment complex. Three weeks after we moved out of where we were previously living, we found out there was a gas leak in the apartment. Unfortunately, It caught on fire and exploded. If we had still been living there, all three of us would have been burned alive. The protection and hand of God was on our lives, another miracle took place, and God gets all of the Glory. The devil wanted to destroy all three of us because of the calling of God on our lives. The devil wants to destroy you because of the calling of God on your life. The Bible says "thanks be to God who always leads us into triumph in Christ Jesus." I believe in miracles, I believe that they are real and available for anybody who puts their faith in Jesus Christ. Nothing is impossible with God to those who believe!

From the age of seven to eighteen years old I was raised in New York and New Jersey. Both of my parents around that time were officers in the Salvation Army and pastored a Church in Newark, NJ and I praise God that season of life.

From the age of seven to twelve, I developed a passion for basketball and music. I stuck with those passions and improved each year and things seemed to be going pretty well. When I was twelve up until eighteen years of age, I kept going strong with basketball and music but also developed some bad habits. These bad habits were developed due to negative influences, peer pressure, and my own personal bad decisions. I dealt with pride, drugs, alcohol, fighting, profanity, immorality, going to house parties and clubs. My life was headed in the wrong direction and I did not have a clue as I thought I was invincible and unstoppable.

Towards the end of my senior year of high school, I looked at my mom, pointed at her and said, "I do not want to live for Jesus and I will never attend a

Christian University." I told her "I am going to do what I want to do and live it up," I intended on playing basketball at a secular party college after I graduated high school. I had plans to go to the NBA or play professional basketball overseas. I wanted to invest the money I made playing professional basketball into a negative rap career and open nightclubs across the United States.

I had the mindset that maybe, just maybe, I would surrender my heart to Jesus Christ when I was seventy years old or something, if ever. Through my high school career, things were only getting worse and more extreme, from the partying, to the drinking alcohol, throwing parties, getting kicked out of schools, etc.

All of a sudden towards the end of my senior year, for some reason I started feeling convicted every time I did something I knew I was not supposed to...

CHAPTER 2

DO NOT BE AFRAID HEAVEN IS REAL

In 2007 towards the end of my senior year of High School, I went to sleep like any regular night. Little did I know that God, the creator of the Universe, was going to reveal something to me so beautiful that I can not fully express it with words. I remember it like it was yesterday as I closed my eyes and my spirit came out of my body. I saw my body laying down on my bed. I walked right through my bedroom wall and ended up outside. As I was outside, I kept on walking and out of nowhere, I felt a tangible energy that I have never felt before. This tangible energy felt radically amazing. I felt it from the top of my head to the soles of my feet on the backside of my spiritual body.

It felt so amazing it literally felt like supernatural tangible joy, peace, excitement, and hope were tickling me. It felt glorious, so glorious that I had to see what it was, so I slowly turned around. As I slowly turned around, this beautiful, majestic, glorious, bright light began to penetrate through the side of my spiritual body. I immediately found out that this glorious light was causing this amazing tangible heavenly tickling sensation that was so pleasurable that I cannot express it with words. The more I shifted and slowly turned my body towards this glorious majestic light, the more it penetrated right through my entire spiritual body.

As I continued to slowly shift towards this glorious light, it reminded me of a sun-ray. It resembled a sun-ray that you see when clouds and sunlight come in contact with each other at the right angle. So I continued to shift in the direction of this glorious light slowly and the more I turned the more it began to penetrate through my spiritual body. I could literally feel every bit of it slowly going through me and it felt so amazing. I have never felt something quite this glorious. I was so excited to see where this glorious light was coming from. With squinted eyes as I was still shifting my spiritual body, afar off I could see that the eternal glorious rays of light were coming from a supernatural, glorious, and beautiful golden city.

As I finally shifted my body one hundred and eighty degrees, I saw that the golden city had a beautiful skyline afar off. Right at the moment when I turned completely towards this glorious light, it penetrated through my entire spiritual body and it fully consumed me. Within a flash, my spiritual body was translated to the middle of this glorious, majestic, golden city. The streets were paved with beautiful golden bricks and the buildings were huge, made out of gold, crystals, different diamonds and rubies. This glorious, tangible light and glory was shooting out of everything and everywhere. It continually penetrated right through my spiritual body and I could feel every ounce of it.

Once again, the joy, peace, pleasure, and excitement I experienced and felt was so strong that it cannot be fully expressed through words. I was in total awe like a ten year old boy would be if he had been given a half a million dollar shopping spree to a massive toy store, with fifteen eighteen-wheeler trucks parked outside ready to haul them to his house, while hundreds of people waited there to help him assemble them, so he could play with them forever, metaphorically speaking. I was supernaturally excited, ecstatic, and in awe of God's glory. Within that same moment that I was translated to this majestic, golden city, I immediately began to run, jump, dance, and scream out, "Heaven is real! Heaven is real! Heaven is real! God's grace is real! Jesus Christ is real! The Holy Spirit is real! Forgiveness is real! God's love is real! The things of God are real! God is real! Heaven is real!"

As I continued to explore this supernatural amazing golden city, out of nowhere this little cloud appeared right in front of my face. It looked to be the size of a soccer ball. As I looked at it, I was able to see three people in this little cloud. Out of the three people,

I could only recognize one of the faces, the one that was in the middle. He was one of my friends from school growing up who I was very close to. Around him was a dark fog, so dark I could barely paint out his face. It appeared to be something like an abyss that they were in.

As I was looking into the little cloud at my close friend, the only way I can explain it is that I could not feel his pain, but I could see his pain. I saw eternal sadness and loneliness in the cloud. I saw depression, anxiety, anger, and eternal separation from the true living God. In the cloud, I saw fear and hopelessness. My close friend in this little cloud in front of me looked into my eyes and yelled out, "Big C, how come you never told me about Jesus Christ?! How come you never told me about His supernatural love?! How come you never reached out to me and introduced me to the Savior of Humanity?!" He said, "How come you never told me about forgiveness of sins, salvation, eternal life, and the grace of God received through repenting of sins and faith in Jesus Christ?! How come you never told me about having a personal relationship with God?! Now I have to stay here in this dark abyss forever with nobody to get me out!" He yelled it out at the top of his lungs with anger in his voice.

Then out of nowhere in Heaven, this little cloud in front of me the size of a soccer ball that I was looking at vanished. I then went back to running, dancing, rejoicing, praising God, and exploring this beautiful, glorious, majestic, crystal golden city. As I was rejoicing in Heaven suddenly, within a flash, my spiritual body translated back into my physical body that was laying on my bed in my room. I suddenly woke up around seven am laughing uncontrollably with explosive joy bubbling out of my belly. I felt exactly what I felt in Heaven surging through my body when I woke up. I felt tangible joy, peace, excitement, and hope all over me and in me. I felt supernatural strength as if I could rip a tree out of the ground.

I leaped off of my bed and opened my bedroom door. I got a hold of my mom, looked in her eyes, and said, "Mom, God took me to Heaven!" She looked into my eyes and said, "Praise God, I believe it! After all, me and your dad have been praying that you would undeniably encounter God." She said, "We literally prayed that God would take you to Heaven through some kind of divine God-given vision or dream." Little did I know that this was going to be the beginning of something amazing. At the time I had no idea that this was going to lead me into being engrafted and recruited into God's family and army through the repentance of and turning away from my sins, by grace through faith in Jesus Christ as the Lord and Savior of my life.

God-Given Interpretation:

After having this divine, God-given dream, out-of-body experience where God showed me Heaven, my life was literally impacted forever. To tell you the truth, over the years I am still getting further interpretation from all of these God-given dreams and visions. Every time I preach and share this dream, I feel like I just had it yesternight. I often think about this divine encounter and it always gives me chills and encourages me in several ways. I will break down parts of my dream of heaven and what they represent to me in the following paragraphs.

The part when my spirit came out of my body and I walked outside and began to turn around to see what was causing the tangible joy, peace, and hope on the backside of my spiritual body, to me represents turning my back on the things and ways of this world. It represented me turning my back on the devil and sin. Me turning towards the light symbolizes me shifting to Jesus Christ and turning to the things of God, turning to the Kingdom of God, His calling, purpose, and destiny for my life. It represents the start of my personal relationship with God. The part where I completely turned around one hundred and eighty degrees, right before I translated to Heaven, is symbolic of me shifting my focus on the Kingdom of God. It represents me completely fixing my eyes on Jesus Christ, the author and the finisher of our faith. This also symbolizes me fully surrendering my life to Jesus and being consumed with the Kingdom of God and great commission. It represents me being fully committed to living a life of prayer and worship unto God, a life where the Word of God is final authority, my identity is in Christ, and being fully surrendered to and rooted in Him.

God's eternal love, peace, true joy and hope that I felt in Heaven represents the emotions of Heaven that we can tap into here on earth through a personal relationship with Jesus. Those divine feelings that I felt in Heaven represented the fruits of the Holy Spirit which we have access to through a personal relationship with God.

This dream of Heaven and out-of-body experience supernaturally impacted my life. It set the tone and pace for my life, thrusting me into a personal relationship with God. This divine encounter opened up my heart to where soon after this dream I surrendered my heart to Jesus. I've been living for God with everything in me with no regrets ever since. Surrendering my heart to JESUS is the best decision I ever made. Each dream in this book and different chapters has a specific message from God to encourage you in the days we are living in. Let this Heaven dream encourage you to know that Heaven is a real place and that eternity is real. The peace, joy, and hope that I experienced in Heaven that cannot be expressed with words, can be experienced here on earth by grace through faith in Jesus Christ. They can be tapped into, but only through a personal relationship with God and His Holy Spirit.

There are a lot of people who are depressed, sad, angry, filled with anxiety, and fear, carrying unforgiveness. I want to encourage you to not be afraid, because Heaven is real; it is a real place. God loves you and your life is so valuable to God. God sent His son Jesus Christ to live for you, shed His perfect blood for you, die for you, and resurrect from the dead for you. He did this so that you could be forgiven of your sins and become a brand new creation in Christ Jesus. He sent Jesus so you could receive eternal salvation, become His Child, and begin a glorious personal relationship with Him. He desires a relationship with you that is full of joy and everlasting peace, one that surpasses human reasoning. There is a divine hope that only comes from the Lord Jesus Christ.

Do not be afraid, Heaven is real...run to Jesus! God's arms are wide open and ready to receive you with His love. By repenting of sins and putting faith in Jesus Christ as your Lord and Savior, you can begin a glorious personal relationship with Him...

Do not be afraid…

Heaven is real…

RUN to JESUS…

God's arms are wide open…

And ready to receive you…

With love.

CHAPTER 3

THE MIRACULOUS JOURNEY CONTINUES

After my first trip to Heaven, my life was forever impacted. My view on life completely changed. After this divine encounter, I came to the reality with no doubt in me, that the Bible is true, God is real, Jesus

Christ is real, the Holy Spirit is real, Heaven is real, hell is real, and the things of God are real. I now knew that I was born and alive on this earth for a greater purpose. At the end of my senior year, I decided that I would be okay with playing basketball for a Christian University. I made the decision that I was going to pursue playing basketball for Oral Roberts University, located in Tulsa Oklahoma. Everything was looking positive so I moved to Tulsa that summer after graduating from St. Mary's High School, shortly after my first trip to Heaven. Shortly after arriving in Tulsa, I was practicing with the ORU Basketball Team and everything was looking good. Out of nowhere, I was informed that playing basketball for Oral Roberts University was not going to work out for a couple of different reasons. At the time I was frustrated and angry because I really wanted to play division one basketball straight out of High School. There were some other opportunities I had but they were outside of the State of Oklahoma.

Since I was already living in Tulsa Oklahoma, I decided to look at options that would allow me to play basketball in the State of Oklahoma. I received an opportunity that same week to play basketball for Rhema Bible Training College. I also found out that my credits would transfer to ORU after two years at Rhema, so I would still be able to pursue playing basketball at ORU after I graduated from Rhema Bible Training College. Although I had already experienced my first encounter of going to Heaven and God opening my eyes to the reality of the spiritual truths concerning Him, His Word, Heaven, hell, and living on Earth for a greater purpose, etc., I still was not fully saturated in His love, nor had I fully committed my life or surrendered my heart to Him and His will yet. I was still willingly involved in some sin and practiced some bad habits. You see, knowing that God is real and fully surrendering your life to Him and His will are two different things. God's plans and purposes for our lives could only come to pass through a life that is fully surrendered to Him.

Around the time of making my decision to play basketball at Rhema Bible Training College, I attended a dance club downtown Tulsa with some people that I had met. This one night in particular at the club, I almost got into a fight with somebody that was in a gang who was disrespecting one of the girls that came with our group. As the club closed that night, and I was in the parking lot in my car about to leave, someone told me that there was a person with a gun roaming the parking lot looking for someone. I did what most people would do in that situation. I put my foot on the gas and exited the parking lot. Who knows what could have taken place that night, but one thing I do know for sure is that the protection of God was on me. I got invited to that same nightclub that same week. Out of nowhere, I had a sudden strong feeling within me not to go. My phone was ringing, people were texting me, some even begging me to go that night. I called some people back telling them that I was not going to the nightclub and that I was going to stay home. The next day I saw on the local news that that same night somebody pulled out a gun and started shooting inside the club. Unfortunately, a young person got hit with a bullet that night and died. He was at the wrong place, at the wrong time, with the wrong people. Hearing about the shooting the next day shocked me. I must say that this life-and-death moment put it into a reality that the nightlife, the fast life, a life of habitual sin, is not worth living. It is not worth your destiny, and certainly not worth the people you are called to reach. It is not worth what you were born to do, or worth the bright future that God has planned for you. The truth is that could have been me that night that got shot and killed at the club.

Just like that, I could have missed out on my God-given destiny and God's plan for my life. I could have missed out on the purposes and blessings of God. I could have missed out on making a difference with my life on this planet for Him. The shooting that happened at the nightclub was another pivotal moment in my life. That Sunday I went to Rhema Bible Church and sat in on the service. My heart was completely opened and every word was piercing my soul. At the end of his message, Pastor Kenneth Hagin gave an altar call to anybody who wanted to surrender their heart to Jesus Christ, repent of sins, and put their faith in Jesus Christ as Lord and Savior of their lives. I was sitting in the back and my heart rate began to go up. I felt Jesus knocking on the door of my heart. Pastor

Hagin said during the altar call, "If that is you, I want you to stand up and come down to the front of the church." There were thousands of people in attendance. At that exact moment, I stood up boldly and walked to the front. That day in 2007 I repented of my sins and put my faith in Jesus Christ as Lord and Savior of my life, and surrendered my heart to Him. To God be all the glory, honor, and praise! It was an unforgettable moment. Around that time I officially decided to play basketball for Rhema Training Bible College for two years and then continue to pursue my Basketball Career by transferring to ORU. Then after playing basketball at ORU, I was going to pursue a contract with an NBA team or play professional basketball somewhere overseas.

Little did I know that during the first couple of months of my freshman year at Rhema Bible Training College, I was going to encounter God in ways I never thought or imagined. I began to receive a personal revelation of how much God loves me and I began to see things in the Bible that I never saw before. I began to catch a revelation that living for God is an opportunity, a privilege, a joy and pleasure. It is fun and it is something that we get to do. I began to catch the revelation of grace, faith, and God's love. My eyes began to open to the true divine beauty of repenting of sins, turning away from sins, and living a surrendered life to Jesus Christ. I also began to receive different miracles in my own life. Not only that but I never saw people so passionate about God and His plan for their lives all in one place. From the coaches, different players on the basketball team, to the students. It was just an awesome experience, something I had never seen before, and I was in amazement.

My first year at Rhema Bible Training College was a monumental year in my life. Literally, everything was taken to the next level. My life was revolutionized because of the personal decision that I made to honor God with my life, my heart, thoughts, words, lifestyle, etc. God is divine, He is strategic, and He obviously knew what He was doing. Being that I was at a Bible College, there could not have been a better place for me to be at that moment in my life. While playing basketball, I was going to get trained at a Bible College, get disciplined in the things of God, and equipped to make a difference for Him in this world. Metaphorically speaking, it was like a soldier at a training center getting equipped with all the weaponry and skills that he needed to be effective in a war against the enemy.

CHAPTER 4

UNDERSTANDING THE BIGGER PICTURE

My second year of Bible College was an amazing year with great experiences, impartations from God's Holy Spirit, and encounters with God. I had no idea that this was going to be the year that would play a huge role in directing the rest of my life. My passion for God was growing by the day more and more. Divine revelations of what Jesus Christ did, who He is, and how He still is alive were taking place. I was becoming more conscious of the reality of who I am in Christ Jesus, how my identity is in Him, and how I no longer live but Christ lives in me.

I began to realize that God wanted His Holy Word, the Bible, to be the final authority in my life. I began to learn about repentance of sins, forgiveness, faith, grace, and the love of God. I began to learn what it means to live a life that glorifies God. I began to see that Christianity is a personal relationship with God by grace through faith in God's only begotten Son Jesus Christ, through His Holy Spirit.

Finally, I was beginning to see and grab ahold of the bigger picture, like why I am alive and breathing, and what my purpose is. My eyes opened up to the truth of what prayer is and how it is simply communicating with God. God showed me that He is always communicating. He communicates through His Holy Spirit whom I received after accepting Jesus Christ as my Lord and the Savior of my life. He communicates through His Holy Spirit through an inward witness, an inward prompting and internal peace. There is a chapter on prayer later in the book where we go a little deeper on this topic. He communicates through His written Word, the Bible, visions, dreams, people, miracles, signs, and wonders. No matter how He speaks to you, it always bears witness with His Holy Spirit inside of you, and it will always line up with His Word.

He is always speaking and He is a personal God who is madly in love with us. As I was reading the Bible one night I saw that God communicated to Joseph through a dream concerning Mary. Right when Joseph was contemplating leaving Mary, Joseph had a dream. In this dream, God used one of His Angels to tell Joseph not to leave Mary. In Matthew 1:20, this Angel told Joseph that God's Holy Spirit impregnated Mary. That night Joseph was brought to peace because of that dream God used to communicate to him. The result was Joseph not leaving Mary and not too long after that, God communicated to Joseph again in a dream through an Angel to leave Jerusalem to go to Egypt.

The reason was King Herod was going to kill all the children under the age of two because he heard the rumor of Jesus Christ, The King of the Jews, being born. My point is that God used a dream to communicate to Joseph concerning two big decisions that changed the destiny of the entire human race. If God spoke to Joseph through a dream on something this significant, He could still speak to any of His children through a dream or vision today. Not only that, but in many different places in the Bible, Old and New Testament, we see where God communicated to people through dreams and visions. God is the same yesterday, today, and forever. If He did it before, He can do it again. There is a divine purpose behind everything God says, does, and communicates.

How can you know if it is really God communicating with you? Well, it is very simple.

Seven Biblical Truths About the Voice of God

#1 When God speaks to you it always lines up with His Holy Word, the Bible.

#2 When God speaks to you it bears witness with God's Holy Spirit on the inside of you.

#3 Often when God speaks to you through a life-altering dream nobody can convince you that it was not God speaking to you.

#4 When God speaks to you in general, there is a knowing on the side of you that it was Him speaking.

#5 When God speaks to you, it inspires you, edifies you, encourages you, corrects you, exhorts you, and empowers you.

#5 When God speaks to you it is not so you can feel like you are better than other people. When He speaks, it is so you can get to know Him more and be encouraged to do what He called you to do and be who He called you to be, all for His Glory. He communicates to you so you can get to know Him on a deeper level and build a personal relationship with Him.

#6 It is key to remember that the number one way God speaks to His Children is through the Bible, His Word. The second is through His inward witness and inward prompting that can come through a still, small voice on the inside of you.

#7 As our personal relationship with God grows through prayer, reading the Bible, Worshiping Him, etc., our ability to hear His voice grows and it becomes more clear. As our relationship with God grows, we also grow in the beauty of obeying and being faithful to His voice. We grow in the ability to follow His voice with a corresponding action, or obedience. God desires that we enjoy Him, that we embrace Him with gratitude, that we live from Him, live in awe of Him, and that we are faithful to His voice. He is a good, good Father and we are His beloved children in Christ Jesus.

Beginning to Understand The Bigger Picture

#1 You were created to personally know God, to praise God, to worship God, and to Glorify God.

How do you do this? You can only do this by allowing His Love for you and everything He made available at the cross for you to be your fuel and gasoline. You must begin to read the Bible out of a personal relationship with God, from the position of being loved, saved, forgiven, and righteous in Christ Jesus. Do not simply read it just to read it, but read it with the intention of eating it, drinking it, and breathing it in. Read the Word with faith and reverence, knowing that it is tangible and living. The Bible is the breath and word of God. We build a relationship with God by talking to God and by letting words of praise and worship come out of our hearts and through our lips unto Him. We do this by allowing our hearts, thoughts, words, and lifestyle to be pleasing to Him. We should live our lives in a way that is an act of worship unto Him in Spirit and in truth. Everything we do, we do unto the Lord. Everything we do, we do it in the name of Jesus Christ. Everything we do, we do in Spirit and in truth. Hallelujah!

#2 You were created to edify and encourage the people in the Kingdom of God. Remember that the only people who are children of God and in the Kingdom of God are those who have repented of their sins and believed with their heart in Jesus Christ as Lord and Savior of their life.

How do you edify and encourage people in the Kingdom of God? You can do this by communicating Biblical truths of God with other children of God, from a place of being rooted in His love. However, make sure to not argue about the truths of God with others. God does not desire that we argue and debate about His Word. He desires that we embrace His Word together as His Children, in unity. He wants us to worship Him together and celebrate people in the Kingdom of God, cheering them on, and refrain from being jealous when He elevates and opens a door for another person. Always remember that it is a joy, pleasure, and privilege to be in the Kingdom of God. We ought to encourage one another, love one another, respect one another, and celebrate one another. We are called to help one another and embrace one another in the love of God, just as we have been embraced and loved by Him.

#3 You were created to make Him known, to expand, and grow the Kingdom of God.

We put this into practice through preaching, teaching, living, and demonstrating the glorious Gospel of Jesus Christ, out of our personal relationship with Him. We do this through allowing God's glory to shine through our heart's motives, thoughts, words, actions, gifts, and talents. We must choose to accept the calling God has placed on our lives, and no matter what calling that is, we are all called to be full-time Christians that bear eternal fruit that glorifies Him. We are called to be fully devoted followers of Jesus Christ and live our lives out of a personal relationship with Him. We must live our lives in a way where people are drawn to Christ. We are called to joyfully live one day at a time with Jesus, putting all of our trust in Him, as we yield to the voice of the Holy Spirit.

As I was being saturated with all of these beautiful supernatural "Biblical Truths" towards the end of my second year of Bible College, little did I know what was going to happen after I graduated from Rhema Bible Training College going into my first year at Oral Roberts University.

CHAPTER 5
THE CLIFF, OCEAN OF FIRE, AND RAPTURE

As I laid my head on my pillow to go to sleep, I had no idea what God was about to reveal to me as I slept. The moment I closed my physical eyes, my spiritual eyes opened up. In this dream, I was on a huge cliff the size of the grand canyon, except there was no canyon. It was just a cliff, and in front of me there were millions and millions of young people.

Everyone was dressed like they were at some kind of citywide pool party, dance club, or outdoor rave festival. The women were dressed in bikinis or stripper-like mini skirts. The men were dressed in swim shorts or dress shirts without ties, with their chests showing, and jeans. Some were drinking alcohol, others were smoking weed. There were drugs everywhere with sexual dancing taking place. There seemed to be music playing, although I could not hear it for some reason. They looked like they were having the time of their lives, everyone appeared to be radically enjoying themselves.

I noticed the only thing that was holding everybody together was two chained handrails, one on the left side and one on the right side, miles apart. All of this was happening so fast I decided to take a look back to see what was behind me. As I slowly turned around, I didn't realize how close I was to the edge of this cliff. I immediately was shocked when I saw what was on the other side of this cliff. I saw the biggest ocean I have ever seen in my life. The only thing different was it was not an ocean of water, it was an ocean of fire and lava.

As I turned back around towards the millions of people, I realized that all of them were going to jump off of the cliff and into this ocean of fire and lava. My concern skyrocketed because I knew none of them knew what they were going to jump into. I turned around one more time and took a quick look at the bottom of the ocean. As I looked I saw a huge disgusting hand with curly, nasty nails at the bottom. I could only see the hand as the waters rocked back and forth violently and uncontrollably. The hand was huge. Words cannot fully describe the vividness of all that was taking place, but I will continue to share.

Out of nowhere, faith began to arise in me and I decided I was going to do whatever it took to warn these people of what they were about to jump into. Right when I was going to speak to the first person, the loudest trumpet blast I have ever heard in my life went off. As the trumpet blew, the millions of people in front of me began to jump off of the cliff. They jumped off the cliff as if they were jumping off of a diving board into some big pool at a water park. They were laughing as they jumped, as if they were having fun and had no idea what they were jumping into. Once they jumped, their eyes opened up to what they were jumping into, but by then it was too late. They fell into the ocean of fire right into the hand (the devil's hand). As they fell down they yelled and screamed at the top of their lungs. I could hear anger, fear, and anxiety in their voices. They were yelling for help as they hit the lava and fire. They were burned alive and died.

In my dream, this was all happening so fast, as people were running by me and jumping off. I immediately grabbed the first person closest to me that was going to jump. The moment I did I had a supernatural grip on him and he could not get away from my grip even if he wanted to. I looked right into his eyes and told him, "Don't jump! There is an ocean of fire and lava on the other side of this cliff!" As I turned his body and head towards the ocean of fire and lava to show him what he was going to jump into, his eyes immediately opened up and he was awoken to the reality of what he was about to jump into. He was excited, freaked out, and shocked because he just got saved from the ocean of fire. At that exact moment, I told him, "Let's get to work, let's grab, and save as many people as we can! And let's do it as fast as we can!" I told him to grab people and show them the ocean of fire so they could be awoken to the truth of what they were about to jump into. I said, "Let's save as many lives as we can, let's do this!" All of this was happening so quickly, and as I was sharing this with him, hundreds of thousands were jumping off the cliff and dying in the ocean of fire and lava.

We started grabbing and saving as many people as we could. It felt like I was in some kind of Oscar-winning action movie. We were grabbing people left and right as fast as we could. Everybody that was awoken to the truth received the same supernatural power and strength to grab people like I did. The supernatural power was only available to grab them to show them what they were jumping into so they could be awoken to the truth, so they could live and not die.

All of a sudden, the loudest trumpet sound went off again. Even though many jumped off and died there were still many that had not jumped yet. Like robots, everybody on the cliff stopped jumping and went back to partying on the cliff as if they were at some big citywide party or rave. The amazingly beautiful thing was that by this point, many were awoken to the truth and saved. I called and brought together all of the people that we saved from jumping off the cliff into the ocean of fire. I told all of them, "Look, the trumpet is about to blow again! And when it does, the people are going to start jumping off the cliff into the ocean of fire!" Even though we saved thousands, there were still thousands that died. I looked at those who were still alive and reminded them that everybody on the cliff was blinded to what they were about to jump into. I encouraged them and said, "God is with you and He has given you the power to grab them and save them!"

I told them, "You can do it through the strength of Christ! The moment the trumpet blasts, start grabbing and saving people!" As I was talking to the group that was saved, suddenly the trumpet blasted again and everybody on the cliff started jumping. I remember this cycle of trumpet blasts happened around ten to fourteen times total. Every single time the trumpet blasted, the people started jumping off. And then when the trumpet blasted again, the people stopped jumping. Eventually the number of people saved kept growing and growing. Even though millions had died, we saved millions by the final trumpet blast. We finally had enough people saved to cover the two mile radius on the Cliff.

So the trumpet blew again and everybody went back to partying on the Cliff. Somehow all the people that were saved could hear me at the same time. I looked at all of them and warned them, "The trumpet is going to blow again! This time before it does, let's all link our arms so they cannot pass us." As we did this, once again that extremely loud trumpet blast went off. Everybody started to run and try to jump off of the cliff. This time, however, they could not jump off because we created a barrier with our linked arms that was made out of all the people that were saved covering the cliff. All of a sudden the most glorious, majestic, energizing light of glory cracked and broke through the dark sky right in front of us. All of the people who were facing us trying to jump off the cliff could not do so because of our human barrier. Immediately they all turned around and together we all marched towards this huge, glorious, majestic, energizing light of Glory. As we did, it consumed all of us and we were raptured in this glorious, majestic light that broke through the sky, shining directly down on us.

God-Given Interpretation

This dream put a fire in my bones from heaven to reach my generation with the glorious Gospel of Jesus Christ. No matter the cost, I determined I was going to do whatever it took to expose the devil and unveil the Kingdom of God. I want to encourage you before I go into the interpretation of this dream which is pretty much self-explanatory. The second part of this book is loaded with spiritual weaponry and biblical truth that will equip you and make you a threat to the devil. By reading this entire God-given book you will be equipped with a Kingdom of God foundation that you will be able to build on enabling you to make an eternal impact with your life on this world. This book is simply a Kingdom of God resource made available to you. The most important Book for you to read, however, is the Bible, the living Word of God.

As I continue with the interpretation of this chapter, know that it is hard to fully express what I saw and felt with words. It was so real, so authentic, and so tangible. I will try to communicate the interpretation through in simple terms. I know the Holy Spirit will also give you interpretation and fill you with fire as you read this dream several times over and over. Here is the interpretation that God has given to me. The young people on the cliff represented this current generation. As they were partying, drinking, smoking, doing immoral things on the cliff, this represented the sin and iniquity that many are living in. This includes sinning against God, sinning against their bodies, and sinning in general. Them being on the cliff not knowing there was an ocean of fire down below, represented people being blinded by the danger of sin and the lies of satan, not knowing their lives were on the line. The generation on the cliff, the millions in sin thinking that they were having the "time of their lives," represents people being deceived by the devil. It symbolizes the people who do not know that satan is about to take their lives and bring them to hell forever, where they will be eternally separated from God.

The hand at the bottom of the ocean with distorted curly nails, that you could only see when the violent waters of fire and lava shook back and forth, represents satan's hand waiting for this generation to die in sin. That is the devil waiting for them to fall right into his hand and be eternally separated from the true living God. This includes eternal torture, torment, experiencing of pain, anxiety, fear, forever loneliness, and depression. The trumpet blasting and the generation jumping off the cliff into the ocean of fire right into the hand of satan, represents those of this generation that are consumed in sin thinking they are having the "time of their lives," dying in sin. They are completely deceived, falling right into satan's hand, into hell, where they are tormented, tortured, and separated from God forever.

The trumpet blasts represented several things and I am still getting deeper revelation on them. The trumpet would blast and then stop, and the people would begin jumping when it blasted again. That represented how we have a window of time to reach this lost, dying, and deceived generation with the glorious Gospel of Jesus Christ. This portrays the end-time birth pains taking place preceding the coming of Christ, which you can read about in Matthew 24. This also reminds us to not take our time here on earth lightly. As we live in these last days, the reality is things are going to continue to get wilder with tornadoes and earthquakes, and viruses spreading across the earth. You can read Isaiah 60: 1-3 to see what I am referring to. God does not desire that we remain asleep in these last days; He desires that we come together as the body of Christ, and that we are unified on the behalf of the kingdom of God. He wants us to do whatever it takes to point people to Him, encourage people to repent of their sins, and put their faith in Jesus. We must help people to build a relationship with God, and get to know them on a personal basis, while also making Him known. We are called to step out in whatever way we can to be the hands and feet of Jesus, a tangible expression of God's heart on the earth.

Continuing with the cliff dream, when the people who were saved began grabbing others before they jumped off and showed them what they were going to jump into, that represented sharing the Gospel of Jesus Christ with the lost. This includes sharing the dangers of sin, exposing the devil's lies and deceptions. It represented the unveiling of the beauty of Jesus Christ and the power of the blood that He shed. It represented showing them the way out by exposing the lies of satan and revealing the beautiful truth of God in Christ Jesus. The part when their eyes were opened up and they did not jump, and started to reach out and save people, represented people repenting of sins and putting their faith in Jesus Christ as their Lord and savior. That represented people surrendering their hearts to Jesus Christ and becoming followers of Jesus Christ. That is symbolic of people getting saved and stepping out to reach the lost with the same message that saved them, the Gospel.

In the dream, we eventually got enough people to cover the entire radius of the cliff and we began to lock arms. That represented the body of Christ unifying and coming together for the sake of our generation being saved. Even though millions died, there were still millions on the cliff. That represents how we are not going to be able to reach or save everybody, but we are at least able to reach *some.* When people tried to jump off but found that they could not because we had a human barrier made out of our locked arms, this represented many people of our generation being saved. This portrays a generation surrendering to Jesus. That same moment as the sky cracked, as the glory and light of God broke through the sky consuming all of us, represented the coming of our Lord Jesus Christ, and the body of Christ on the earth being raptured.

Get excited as we are living in the last days! Do not just sit back and watch a generation die and go to hell. Take your position in Christ Jesus, live a life that glorifies God. Live with heart motives that glorify God. Live with thoughts that glorify God, speak words that glorify God. Live a life that glorifies Him in Spirit and in Truth. I want to encourage you to not blend in with the world. Live a pure and holy life in Christ Jesus, empowered through a personal relationship with Him. Live out of your personal relationship with God; stir up passion for the things of God. Be about what He is about, rise up, take your position, and play your role. God has placed things on the inside of you that this world needs and that this generation needs. The trumpets are blasting. Jesus Christ came, He lived, He shed His blood, He died, defeated satan, demons, sin, death, hell, and the grave. And He resurrected from the dead victorious on the third day!

The blood that He shed was shed for the sins of humanity. Dirty or sinful blood cannot wash away dirty sins; but the perfect, righteous, Holy blood of Jesus Christ, God's only-begotten son, can wash away your sins forever! By repenting of your sins, confessing your sins to God, putting faith in Jesus Christ, and confessing Him as your Lord and Savior, you become a brand new Creation in Christ. Your sins are washed away, God's Holy Spirit comes to live on the inside of you. You get engrafted and birthed into the Kingdom of God and now have the ability of Christ, the identity of Christ, and the authority of Christ. You have the empowerment to live an overcoming life against the devil and have a victorious life in Christ Jesus that glorifies God and brings Heaven to earth.

As you continue to read the Bible and read through the chapters and dreams in this book, I believe God is going to continue to reveal things to you that will put a Holy fire in you. You will experience a radiant, vivid passion in you for the things concerning Him. I believe He will stir up an excitement in you to advance His Kingdom. Get excited! Get excited! Get excited! We are in the last days and you have a part to play. Do not allow anything to put out your passion for the things of God. Go forward…the grand finale Jesus movement has begun!

God wants to save us, forgive us, build a relationship with us; He desires the best for all of us. Out of a vibrant, personal relationship with Him is where we thrive and flourish. Through a life of prayer, worship, and the Bible we can build a personal relationship with Him. From that place is where we live the Gospel and share the Gospel. From that place is where we share our testimony of how Jesus changed our lives. We do it from a personal relationship with Him; our gasoline is His divine love for us, proven through Jesus Christ. You have been chosen for this hour, there are people on the other side of your yes to Jesus. Go forward in His calling knowing that He is with you. Put your faith in JESUS, keep walking in the love of God, keep forgiving, keep believing, keep moving forward in the grace of God! God is going to use your life to reach other people while they still have a heartbeat. You are valuable. You have a part to play. You are loved.

CHAPTER 6
FIST FIGHT WITH THE DEVIL

A couple of years later I had another jaw
dropping encounter that took place. I went to sleep and
God gave me another dream that gave me a greater
glimpse of the power that we have in Christ Jesus. In
the dream, I was inside of a boxing ring sitting on a
chair in the right corner. All of a sudden I heard a bell
ring and I knew the fight had begun. I lifted my head
and looked straight ahead. In front of me on another
side of the ring was the devil in boxing gear. He was the
nastiest looking creature I had ever seen in my life. He
slowly began to walk towards me with his hands up

and ready to fight. I then stood up and began to walk towards him with my hands up and ready to fight.

We eventually got close enough to where we were in striking distance. I hit the devil with a right hook to the face and a jab to the chest. In retaliation, he threw a couple of punches at me and landed them. We went back and forth and I felt every bit of it. I was throwing punches at him and he was throwing punches at me. I started to get frustrated because he was landing hits on me. Then all of sudden I realized I was fighting him loose-handed. For some reason, my hands were not gripped tight. I realized that I was not hitting him with all of the power that was given to me by God through His Holy Spirit, received by grace through faith in Jesus Christ.

Out of nowhere, I gripped my hands as tight as possible. Right when I did, there was supernatural power that released within my entire body. It felt supernaturally amazing, then the devil gave me a right hook but I ducked and he missed me completely. I cocked my right hand back as supernatural power was releasing in my body. I was gripping my fists tightly and I threw a power-packed punch in the center of the face of the defeated devil. The only thing different this time was he fell right on his back fast and hard. He fell so hard that the entire boxing ring shook. After he fell back, he slowly tried to get back up. Right when he did, I cocked my right hand back again and punched him in the face and he fell back again before he could get back up.

He tried to get back up again and again but he could not. Every time he tried, I cocked my arm back with my hand gripped tightly and hit him. In other words, he was on his back and could not get up. Ever since I fully tightened my grip, supernatural power was released in my body, and I was untouchable. Every time I punched the devil from the time my fists were tightened, there was another release of supernatural power. The release of power in my body felt like supernatural joy, peace, hope, and excitement that I could not express fully with words. The more I tightened my grip, the more that supernatural power was released through my entire body. Every time I threw a punch at the devil and hit him it felt so amazing. Then suddenly, I woke up in my bed overflowing with joy, faith, peace, hope, and excitement.

God-Given Dream Interpretation

As I woke up I knew that God was communicating to me through another dream. I asked God, "What does this dream mean, and what is the interpretation?" He then gave it to me. My opponent in the boxing ring wearing a hoodie on his head was the devil. Me and the devil throwing punches at each other represented spiritual warfare against the devil. The devil landing punches on me at the beginning of the fight represented me not using the full authority God gave me by grace through faith in Jesus Christ through His Holy Spirit.

As I gripped my hands, tightly cocked back my right hand, and hit the devil, it represented me tightly grabbing ahold of the promises of God, my privileges, my rights, and the benefits I have as a child of the living God by grace through faith in Jesus Christ. It represents living out of my new identity in Christ Jesus. It is an example of using the authority and weaponry of worshiping God, the weaponry of prayer, reading the

Bible out loud, declaring the word of God in faith, and casting out demons at the Name of Jesus Christ.

The part where the devil tried to get up repeatedly as I hit him without being touched, represented me making the decision to continue to utilize God's power and authority given to me by grace through faith in Jesus Christ. Furthermore, this symbolizes the Holy Spirit enabling me to live in continual victory. We have victory over the devil and are untouched by any of his attacks as we live from a place of our identity in Him and the authority we have in Jesus Christ.

Be encouraged through this dream that God gave me. Be encouraged in the divine truth that Jesus Christ defeated the devil one hundred to zero! Be encouraged knowing that you have God-given authority in Christ Jesus because of your faith in Him. Do not take God's promises for you lightly. Never take the name of Jesus lightly. As a born-again new creation in Christ Jesus, you have the legal right to use the name of Jesus Christ to cast out devils. Through the life, bloodshed, and resurrection of Jesus Christ, the new birth born-again experience was made available to you and me.

When you confess your sins to God, repent of your sins, and put your faith in Jesus Christ as Lord of your life, your sins are washed away, you become a brand new creation, all things become new. You become born of God, born of His incorruptible seed, born of His love, and engrafted into the body of Christ. You become engrafted into the army of God, part of a divine force on the earth that cannot be stopped. God desires that you live out of this new identity in Christ

Jesus. A little later in the book, there is a chapter designated to the divine truth of identifying with Jesus Christ. After you read that chapter and read this chapter again I believe the Holy Spirit of God is going to reveal even more divine truth to you. It is going to motivate you and encourage you to live in the authority and victory that you have in Christ Jesus, so that anytime the devil tries to attack you, you will use everything God has given you in Christ Jesus to keep the devil on his back. This will enable you to live untouched by the enemy.

God desires that you have a Holy Spirit radar filtering the thoughts that you think. Oftentimes the devil tries to attack human beings in the thought realm. You need to have a radar that the moment you detect a thought that should not be in your mind, you use your God-given weaponry and authority in Christ Jesus to destroy that thought. Once again, there is also a chapter later in the book on renewing your mind and the power of words. Know that when you speak the word of God from the first-person in faith, the thought that should not be in your brain is destroyed. That thought evaporates and your mind is renewed. Allow God's love to be the gasoline and driving force of your life. Live by faith in the Lord Jesus Christ. Keep your eyes on JESUS and choose to live in awe of God. Use the authority that God has given you knowing that in Christ you live, move, and have your being.

CHAPTER 7
SECOND TRIP TO HEAVEN

Some years later, God gave me another glimpse of Heaven. I can truly say that all it takes is one encounter with Jesus Christ for someone's life to be transformed and impacted for eternity. Once again, God gave me a second dream of heaven, and little did I know what God was going to communicate to me that night as I went to sleep. I remember it like it was yesterday; I went to sleep that night and the moment I closed my eyes, at the speed of light, my spirit translated to a white room that was full of the glory of God. The whole room was consumed with this glorious light. I felt joy, peace, and hope that cannot be fully expressed with words.

As I turned around there was a younger-looking individual in a white robe radiating with the glory of God. I took a step back and was in awe. As I looked in his eyes I literally could see the glory of the true living God radiating in him, on him, and through him. As I looked at him I asked him, "Do you like it here?" He replied, "I love it here," and smiled with a glorious smile. He said, "It's glorious, it's wonderful, it's awesome, it's amazing." He began to use different magnificent words to describe Heaven. As I looked at him for some reason I asked him in this dream, "Do you know when Jesus Christ is going to return?" This radiating angelic-like being looked at me and quoted a verse in the Bible. He said, "Nobody knows the exact time or day that Jesus Christ is going to return." He said, "This is what I can tell you, there is a gold clock in Heaven and the little hand is at nine o'clock. When that little hand strikes the midnight hour, Jesus Christ is going to return." In the dream he then said, "The time on the earth and the time in Heaven are different. Nobody knows the exact time or day Jesus Christ is going to return other than God." Then he said, "This is what I can tell you, Jesus Christ is coming soon," as he smiled and giggled.

Then out of nowhere, my spirit translated back into my body. As I woke up in my bed, I felt the tangible presence of God, inexpressible joy everlasting, and a divine sense of determination to continue to seek God first, His Kingdom, and His righteousness. I felt a divine motivation to continue to fulfill the call of God on my life and to continue to advance His Kingdom on the earth. My passion to continue to worship God, talk to Him through prayer, and read the Bible, the Word of God, was radically stirred up. I woke up in my bed with more fire and passion from the Holy Spirit to preach, teach, live, and demonstrate the glorious Gospel of Jesus Christ. I was more determined to do whatever I could do with the strength Christ gave me to bring people into the Kingdom of God, disciple them, direct them towards churches, and grow the Kingdom of God.

I want this dream to encourage you and remind you about the divine truth of eternity, the divine truth of Heaven, and the reality that this physical life will not last forever. We are simply passing through this earth. I want to encourage you to invest your life in the Kingdom of God. I want to encourage you in the divine truth that Jesus Christ is coming soon and His radiant body, those who are in Christ Jesus, will be raptured. I want this dream to encourage you in the reality that God wants to use your life to be a light unto this dark world. God wants to flow through your life, out of your relationship with Him. From that divine place of a personal relationship with God is where we are most effective.

I know that as you read these dreams in this book the Holy Spirit is also going to give you divine interpretation and encouragement. Let it encourage you and motivate you in the things of God. Write and journal what God speaks to you. Get excited as we are living in the last days; what a moment to be alive in Christ, what a time to rise up and be the glorious Body of Christ. What a time to live in the fruits of the Holy Spirit and the gifts of the Holy Spirit. What a time to reach this dying and lost generation with the glorious message of Jesus Christ, the Gospel!

If not now, then when? If not you, then who? When do you seek God? Every day. Who do you pray with? Everybody. Where do you share the Gospel? Everywhere. We are the hands and feet of Jesus Christ, a tangible expression of God's Heart on the earth.

Jesus Christ is coming soon...

There are people connected to your yes to JESUS!

Chapter 8

HURTING CHILD HEALED

God has many different ways of reaching His creation. For whatever reason, He chose to reach me through a trip to Heaven, a dream, out-of-body experience. I came to Christ and surrendered my life to Him through that encounter. Ever since I came to Christ, He speaks to me through dreams on a regular basis. The dreams and visions that I put in this book, I included because God confirmed them to me. If you read each dream thoroughly you will see that there is a divine message from the Holy Spirit and a divine impartation to encourage you in different biblical truths for the glory of God.

God gave me this dream some years later and it is powerful. I hosted a concert one night in the city of Tulsa. People came out and were impacted for the glory of God. People surrendered their hearts to Jesus, people were healed and set free from demonic oppression through the power of Jesus Christ. It was another amazing time in the presence of God. After the concert before I went to sleep, I was in a place of radical gratitude and thankfulness, praising God for what He did that night and for all the testimonies. I was simply in a place of joy, peace, and thankfulness. As I went to sleep little did I know what was going to take place...

The moment I went to sleep, suddenly in this dream I found myself on a couch sitting down. I looked to my right and there was a young boy around the age of four or five sitting right next to me. As I looked at him I saw that he was crying, he was dirty, he had cuts on his body, black eyes like he got beat up and his clothes were dirty. It looked like someone dragged this child in the mud. As I looked at him, I was filled with overwhelming compassion. He then looked at me, and I was wondering how he got next to me. All I remember is I took him under my arm and gave him a side hug to try to calm him down. I wanted to help him, I wanted to see him healed.

In this dream as I put my arm around him to hug him, I felt a divine love, compassion, and glorious tangible power from Heaven being released from the inside of me going into his body as I gave him a hug. Out of nowhere, this power that was coming out of my body and going into his body was healing him. His cuts healed up, the dirt on him was washed away with this tangible power, his black eyes were healed immediately, his clothes were clean, he went from sadness to joy, from crying to laughing.

The child was healed completely by the power, love, and compassion of God in Christ Jesus. I then suddenly woke up at three in the morning drenched in the compassion of God, crying tears of compassion. I woke up in tears yet I had joy in my heart. The only way to express it is that I was drenched inside and out in the glorious compassion of God. I immediately began to think about that verse in the Bible where Jesus Christ said he was moved with compassion and he healed many. I was immediately encouraged and reminded of how God desires that you and I are to be moved with compassion when it comes to reaching the lost. He desires that our drive and engine to preach, teach, live and demonstrate the glorious Gospel of Jesus Christ be compassion and divine love for the lost. People are hurting and in need of a Savior and His name is Jesus Christ of Nazareth. The hurting child in the dream represented a dying and hurting generation in need of a loving Savior Jesus Christ. Hugging the child represented being the hands and feet of Jesus, a tangible expression of God's heart on the earth. It is an example of sharing the Gospel of Jesus Christ, encouraging people in the Lord, and fulfilling the great commission. It represented showing the love of Christ, representing Him, helping hurting people, and pointing them to Jesus.

God desires that we are not moved by selfish ambition or prideful motives. He wants us to be fueled by His love, driven, and moved by His compassion. He desires that we serve Him with gladness, moved by pure Christ motives, moved by His love. Be encouraged by this dream, and may the Holy Spirit of God invade every part of you with His divine power of compassion.

The next chapter is geared toward encouraging you and teaching you about God's love for you. You matter, your life is valuable to God, He created you and He knows you best. Only the Creator can satisfy His creation. Only the Maker can fulfill what He made. The rest of this book is aimed toward equipping you with divine, foundational teaching from the word of God. A foundation will be laid for you to be a fruit-producing disciple of Jesus Christ that lives in the fruits and gifts of the Holy Spirit. The next chapters are going to encourage you on the basics of Christianity, equipping you with the basics of God's kingdom, and enabling you to develop a biblical foundation so that you can make an eternal impact with your life on this earth. They will empower you to live a life that glorifies God and cause you to invest in eternity. Get excited because by the time you are done reading this entire book, there will be a Holy Spirit fire burning in you for the things of God that will never be able to be put out.

You are chosen by God. You are loved by God. You are valuable to God. You are embraced by God. You are celebrated by God. You are pursued by God. You are

God's beautiful creation. He desires a relationship with you so much...

He is waiting on you...

You are chosen.

CHAPTER 9
GOD LOVES YOU

God loves you and He proved it by sending His Son Jesus Christ. Jesus Christ was sent by God; He chose to come, He lived, He died, He shed His blood, rose from the dead on the third day victorious, proclaimed the Kingdom of God for forty days, and then ascended into the sky at the right hand of Father God in Heaven. By fulfilling the mission that Father God gave Him, He defeated the devil, sin, death, hell, and He defeated the grave, making redemption available to humanity. This beautiful assignment being fulfilled is the living tangible evidence and proof that you and I have that God loves us. We do not have to wonder if God loves us. Because of what Jesus Christ did, we can know that God loves us. No matter who you are, what you have done, what you have said, or what sin you have committed, GOD LOVES YOU. John 3:16 says that, "God so loved the world that He gave His only begotten Son that whosoever believes in Him shall not perish but have everlasting Life."

This beautiful assignment that Jesus Christ fulfilled also reveals to us and shows us a clear picture that God is for us and not against us. It reveals God's heart towards us. It also shows us that He wants us to prosper in every area of our lives. He wants us to prosper spiritually in our relationship with Him, mentally, emotionally, physically, financially, in our friendships, relationships, and in the passions that He has placed in our hearts. John 10:10 says, "The devil comes to kill, steal, and destroy, but Christ came to give us life and give it to us more abundantly." Also, Jeremiah 29:11 says, "For I know the plans I have for you, declares the Lord, plans to prosper you and not to harm you, plans to give you hope and a future." God is madly in love with us, after all, He created us. He desires a personal relationship with us, and just like a father wants the best for his kids, father God wants the best for us as His Children in Christ Jesus.

It is God's will that His supernatural love fuels and empowers our lives the same way gasoline fuels and empowers a car to run, or the same way jet fuel empowers a plane to fly. God's love is energizing, it is fulfilling, exciting, and full of everlasting life. 1 John 4:19 says, "We love God because He first loved us." In other words, we are fueled and empowered to love and be faithful to God because He loved us first. His love empowers us to worship Him, talk to Him, read His word, speak His word, and share about Jesus Christ and His supernatural love. There is no love greater than the love of God that has been proven through His Son

Jesus Christ. God desires that His love fuels and empowers us to love Him, love ourselves with that God kind of love, and love our neighbors. A revelation of God's love for you proven through Jesus Christ will make you a better everything. It will make you a better mom, a better dad, a better sibling, a better son, a better daughter, a better friend, a better employee, a better disciple of Jesus. A revelation of God's love proven through Jesus will transform your life from the inside out forever.

When you and I choose to live our lives with an ongoing growing revelation of how much God loves us, we are able to do things we normally could not do on our own. For example, when somebody "does you dirty," hurts you, or does you wrong in some kind of way, instead hurting them, or doing them wrong, we respond differently. When God's love for you is your gasoline, you will be able to speak life over them and freely forgive them. Jesus Christ was conscious of Father God's love for Him, and that is one of the reasons He was able to fulfill His mission and assignments from God. When He was on the cross dying, He said, "Father forgive them for they know not what they do," to the people that crucified Him, wanted Him crucified, and rejected Him.

One of the root reasons He was able to do and say that was because He was conscious of how much Father God loved Him. When you have the correct perspective of God and you know that He loves you, know that He is for you, and not against you, you know that He has your back and that He is a good God. When you build your life on the divine truth that God loves you and Jesus Christ proved it, when you build your life on the word of God, you are not moved by anything that comes against you because the foundation that your life is built on is a rock-solid foundation. It is unshakable and cannot be moved.

Christianity is not a set of rules and regulations made to control masses of people with no zeal, no energy, no life, and no passion. Christianity is not a religion. Christianity is a living personal love-relationship with God. It is a personal relationship with the Creator of the Universe. It happens through confessing and repenting of your sins to God, according to 1 John 1:9. It happens by grace through faith in His Son Jesus Christ, as shown in Ephesians 2:8, and through His Holy Spirit, according to Romans 8:11 and 1 Corinthians 6:19. The Holy Spirit comes to live in us after we become born-again, one with Him, re-created brand new creations in Christ Jesus. 2 Corinthians 5:17 says, "Therefore if any man is in Christ, He is a brand new creature: old things are passed away; behold, all things have become new." The Bible is a love letter and the Gospel of Jesus Christ is the greatest eternal love story. You are valuable, you are the apple of God's eyes, the center of His attention. God loves you so much and His Son Jesus Christ tangibly proved it.

Every human has a void on the inside of them. Every person has an emptiness inside of them. Some people try to fill that void on the inside of them with drugs, alcohol, wrong relationships, sin, the things of this world. The reality is none of that could fill that emptiness and void. The ONLY thing that could fully fulfill that void and emptiness on the inside of every human is the love of God, proven through Jesus Christ. The only thing that could fulfill that void is an ongoing growing vibrant personal relationship with God by grace through faith in His Son Jesus Christ, through His Holy Spirit.

If you messed up and sinned against God by lying, cheating, stealing, fornication, immorality, gossip, slander, manipulation, pornography, adultery, drunkenness, or whatever the sin you committed, the reality is that the sins you committed separate you from God. Sin stops you from being able to have a personal relationship with Him. Sin gives demons the legal right to torment your mind and emotions with fear, depression, guilt, shame, anxiety, and the negative list goes on. Sin gives the devil the legal right to even attack your health.

People living in sin and breaking God's laws who reject Jesus Christ and His blood that was shed, have hell secured as their eternal destination after their physical life on earth ends. Hell is a place of never-ending pain, torture, torment, depression, anxiety, fear, shame, guilt, and eternal separation from the true living God. Hell is an eternal jail for those who break God's laws and who reject Jesus Christ and the perfect blood that He shed. That blood was shed so that we could be forgiven of sins, receive salvation, and go to Heaven and eternally be with God when our physical life on earth ends

Heaven is a place of everlasting hope, joy, and peace so strong that it cannot be expressed with words. It is a place where we will eternally be connected to God and His everlasting glorious kingdom. There we will have eternal fellowship and communion with Him. In Heaven we will worship Him and be with the family of God forever. We are simply passing through this earth. Who we put our faith in dictates where we will spend eternity. Who we put our faith in dictates whether we will receive God's Kingdom, righteousness, peace, and joy in the Holy Spirit into our lives here on earth. Who we put our faith in dictates whether we receive Heaven as our eternal destination after our physical life on earth ends.

I want to encourage you to put your faith in Jesus Christ and repent of your sins and begin a personal relationship with God. As you do you will receive GOD'S GLORIOUS REDEMPTION PACKAGE that includes salvation, forgiveness of sins, eternal life, righteousness, new creation identity in Christ, healing, freedom, authority in Christ, sonship, being engrafted into God's Family, and the glorious list goes on. You will learn more about the redemption package and benefits in the next chapter entitled *Identity in Christ*.

Surrender your heart to JESUS. GOD loves you so much... do not run from Him...run to Him...

I encourage you to pray this prayer of salvation and deliverance with me, through faith in Jesus Christ. Be free from the demonic torment and forgiven of your sins. Receive salvation through Christ Jesus today and begin your relationship with Him. If your relationship with God has become cold and dry, rededicate your life to Him today...

PRAYER OF SALVATION AND DELIVERANCE

Confess this prayer with me from your heart by faith: "By faith God, I ask you for the forgiveness of every sin I have ever committed. Forgive me for sinning. Forgive me for opening up doors to demonic activity through sin. I put my faith in your Son Jesus Christ today. I confess with my mouth and believe with my heart that Jesus Christ is my Lord and Savior. I believe that He is your son, I believe that He is the Messiah, I believe that He rose from the dead victorious on the third day. Jesus Christ, I receive your grace, I receive everything you made available through your life, bloodshed, resurrection, and ascension into heaven at the right hand of God. God, forgive me for every person I ever hurt. By faith, I forgive everybody who ever hurt me in Jesus' name. Holy Spirit, I ask that you baptize me, fill me with your love, fire, and with your power. Holy Spirit, I ask you to fill me to overflow. God, I ask you to make my life a demonstration of your grace, love, and power. I cancel and break every demonic chain and stronghold in the Name of Jesus Christ that was attached through the decisions I have made through sins. I command every demonic force entity to leave in the name of Jesus Christ. I dedicate my heart, my mind, my emotions, my body, my life, my house, everything I own to you, Jesus Christ. Holy Spirit, I give you complete access to every aspect of my life. From this day on I will live for you with all of my heart, all of my thoughts, all of my emotions, all of my body, and all of my life, for you are the true living God. My past, present, and future is bright because I have become one with you, Jesus Christ. Hallelujah in the mighty name of Jesus Christ, Amen."

Let these Bible Verses Encourage you

"That if thou shalt confess with thy mouth the Lord Jesus, and shalt believe in thine heart that God hath raised him from the dead, thou shalt be saved." Romans 10:9

"If we confess our sins, he is faithful and just to forgive us our sins, and to cleanse us from all unrighteousness." 1 John 1:9

"For by grace are ye saved through faith; and that not of yourselves: it is the gift of God." Ephesians 2:8-10

"This is the covenant that I will make with them after those days, saith the Lord, I will put my laws into their hearts, and in their minds will I write them."
Hebrew 10:16

"And hope maketh not ashamed; because the love of God is shed abroad in our hearts by the Holy Ghost which is given unto us." Romans 5:5

"Therefore if any man be in Christ, he is a new creature: old things are passed away; behold, all things are become new." 2 Corinthians 5:17

"And now abideth faith, hope, love, these three; but the greatest of these is love." 1st Corinthians 13:13.

"We love him, because he first loved us." 1 John 4:19

"For God so loved the world, that he gave his only begotten Son, that whosoever believeth in him should not perish, but have everlasting life. For God sent not his Son into the world to condemn the world; but that the world through him might be saved." John 3:16-17

"For as many as are led by the Spirit of God, they are the sons of God." Romans 8:14

"Ye are of God, little children, and have overcome them: because greater is he that is in you, than he that is in the world." 1 John 4:4

"And he said unto them, Go ye into all the world, and preach the gospel to every creature." Mark 16:15

In the book of Genesis we see that Adam and Eve disobeyed God's instruction in the garden of Eden by eating the forbidden fruit from the tree of the knowledge of good and evil. By doing this they got kicked out of the garden of Eden and sin came into this world. The world is still suffering thousands of years later because of the decision they made to disobey God.

Jesus Christ, the Son of God, was sent by Father God to redeem humanity. Jesus Christ freely gave up His life for me and you. His perfect blood was shed for the sins of the entire human race. The Bible says in 2 Corinthians 5:21, "He who knew no sin became sin so we can become the righteousness of God in Christ Jesus." Humanity broke God's law through sin, disobedience, but Jesus Christ paid the fine through His life, bloodshed, and resurrection. Even though He paid the fine to receive what He purchased with His blood, there is still an action that needs to be made on our part. That action is believing in Him and putting our faith in Him. That action is confessing our sins, repenting of our sins, and turning away from them. We must accept Jesus Christ and confess Him as our Lord and Savior, believe that He rose from the dead on the third day, believe that He is the Son of God and Messiah, and believe that He is who He says He is.

God is love, according to 1 John 4:8. But He is also Holy and just. That is why He cannot have a personal relationship with those who reject His Son Jesus Christ and reject the perfect blood He shed. God loves you so much and Jesus Christ is the tangible evidence and proof of this divine truth. Allow God's love for you to draw you to your knees. Allow His love for you to convict you of sins and empower you to repent of your sins. Allow God's love for you to radically encourage you. Allow it to motivate you to put your faith in Jesus Christ so you could be forgiven for your sins and become a brand new creation in Christ Jesus. You then can begin a personal, joyful, peaceful, vibrant, relationship with the living God, by grace through faith in Jesus Christ, through His Holy Spirit.

God's love for us is not a license to sin and to break His laws. His love for us is not a license to live however we desire according to our flesh, the impulses of our flesh, and the ways of this world. His love is divine empowerment *not* to sin. His love is a divine enablement to live a righteous, holy, sanctified life in Christ, out of a personal relationship with Him. His love for us is supernatural empowerment to get up and to keep moving forward in the plans and purposes He has for our lives. His divine love for us is supernatural gasoline, fueling us to have an explosive desire to worship Him, to read His word, to talk to Him through prayer, speak His word, and to share our testimony of how He saved us with people. His love empowers us to share the glorious message of Jesus Christ with this hurting world. His love is gasoline to plant Jesus seeds, water Jesus seeds, ultimately enabling us to reap Jesus fruit. What a joy it is to be a carrier of God's divine love.

Faith, hope, and love abide, but the greatest of these is love, according to 1 Corinthians 13:13. Allow God's love to continually be poured into your heart out of your relationship with Him. By worshiping Him, praying, reading the Bible, speaking faith, and sharing the Gospel, you build a personal relationship with Him. This should be done every day, not just once a week. This is something that should also be done throughout the day. It is a pleasure, joy, and an honor to get to know Him and to make Him known. As He pours into you, you can freely pour into those around you. God desires that you live from the inside out through your in-Christ identity and new birth experience, instead of being directed or controlled by the flesh, circumstances, and situations on the outside.

In the next chapter, I will be going more in-depth on the divine truth and reality of your brand new identity in Christ Jesus. I will cover the authority that He has given us to live victorious over darkness and the defeated devil. The second part of this book is developed and geared towards laying a foundation on the basics of Christianity. These chapters are loaded with liquid gold from heaven to encourage you to be who God has called you to be and do what He has called you to do. I can guarantee that by the time you are done reading this book, there will be a Holy Spirit fire, power, and love exploding on the inside of you. This will cause an excitement from Heaven to burn inside your bones to build a relationship with Him, to seek Him, and to advance His Kingdom on the earth, by preaching and living the Glorious Gospel of Jesus Christ.

Chapter 10

IDENTITY IN CHRIST JESUS

In this chapter, I simply want to encourage you in the reality and truth of what took place after you repented of your sins and put your faith in Jesus Christ as Lord and Savior of your life. It is very key for you to understand what it means to identify with Jesus Christ. It is imperative for you to have a clear picture of what that looks like. God desires that you live from your new identity in Christ, that you live from that new place of being one with Him. In the New Testament, you will see the term "in Him," "in whom," and "in Christ," used over one hundred times. God desires that we live conscious of who we are in Christ.

When you confessed your sins, repented of your sins, and put your faith in Jesus Christ as Lord of your life, you became a brand new creation in Christ Jesus. You received a brand new identity. When Adam and Eve disobeyed God's instruction and got kicked out of the garden of Eden, sin came into this world. Unfortunately because of that mistake, every human is born with a sinful nature. That is why you even see kids at an early age disagreeing with and disobeying their parents. The good news is by putting faith in Jesus Christ, our sins are forgiven and washed away. We become born again in Christ; we become born of God, born of His incorruptible seed, and become one with Christ. At that moment we receive God's nature on the inside of us.

A little bit later in this chapter, I will present you with a list of some of your new creation realities in Christ Jesus. God desires that you live out of your new identity in Christ Jesus. He desires that you confess these new realities of who you are in Christ over yourself. Keep these realities at the forefront of your mind. He desires that you live from that place of being in Him. This glorious truth of identifying with Jesus and the perfect blood that He shed enables you to identify with Jesus and not identify with your past mistakes and sins. It does not matter what you did in the past, when you repent of your sins and put your faith in Jesus Christ it is completely forgiven and completely washed away. Jesus Christ paid for your forgiveness with His perfect blood. The Bible says that He who knew no sin became sin that we may become the righteousness of God in Christ Jesus. The Bible says He bore our iniquities on the cross. The Bible says that if you confess your sins to God He is faithful and just to forgive you of your sins. By putting your faith in Jesus Christ and putting your faith in His perfect righteous Holy blood, you can stand blameless, shameless, and righteous in the sight of God in Christ Jesus.

There is a chapter in the Bible where we see a man named Nicodemus talking to Jesus Christ in John 3. Jesus Christ told him, "To see the Kingdom of God you must be born again." Nicodemus was trying to understand, and even asked, "How is this possible?" He said, "I cannot go back into my mother's womb." Jesus said, "You must be born of water and Spirit, you must be born again." What was Jesus referring to? He was talking about your born-again, new-creation identity, in-Christ experience. He was talking about God's Holy Spirit coming to live on the inside of you. He was referring to you becoming one with Him and receiving His new identity, enabling you to be reconciled back to Him and forgiven of your sins. This enables you to be restored and reconciled back to God, allowing you to have a personal relationship with Him.

God desires that you are rooted in this divine truth of identifying with Jesus Christ. He wants you to be so rooted that you realize you do not identify with your past, present, or future. You identify with Jesus Christ of Nazareth. The reality is just because you receive God's nature on the inside of you, does not mean that you are never going to make a mistake again. The reality is we live in a fallen world and you still have a flesh and a mind. This is why the apostle Paul said in Romans 12:2 that we are transformed by the renewing of our minds. In this chapter, I am simply focusing on the basic and yet powerful truth of identifying with Jesus.

There is a chapter later in the book where I focus on the power of renewing your mind, but I will share a little on this topic now. Just because your spirit becomes born again and one with Christ and you receive a new creation identity in Him, does not mean that your mind gets born-again. The reality is your mind still has to be renewed. You still have to sacrifice your flesh and yield to God's Holy Spirit. You still have to not be directed by fleshly impulses. It is key to understand that it is not in your own ability, but rather out of your relationship with Him. It is through your identity in Christ, His ability flowing through you. It is by using the weapon of renewing the mind with the word of God. You do this by keeping a "filter" on your brain, that filter being the word of God. As you do, you will develop a habit of living out of your new identity in Christ, living out of your relationship with God, and not yielding to fleshly impulses, whatever that may be.

God desires that we are disciplined in the area of reminding ourselves and renewing our minds with new creation realities in Christ Jesus. Here is a list of some of your new realities in Christ Jesus. This is who you are; you are not your past, you are a born-again spirit in Christ Jesus. You are one with Him.

New Creation, in-Christ Identity List

Child of God

Forgiven

Loved

Righteous (in right-standing with God)

Citizen of heaven

Temple of the Holy Spirit

God becomes your Father

Reconciled back to God

Born into the family of God

Engrafted into the army of God

Saved

Eternal life

Blameless

Shameless

Guiltless

Restored

Healed

Free from the curse of the Old Testament law

Empowered

Equipped

Renewed

Accepted

Valued

Verified

Validated

Sealed With God's promise

Blessed

Personal access to the true Living God

The glorious, beautiful list is endless. This is your new identity in Christ Jesus. This is who you are, this is what you identify with. This is where you live out of and where you live from. It is a blessing from the true living God, it is a free GIFT made available through JESUS. Never take your identity in Christ Jesus lightly. Praise God for it! He loves us so much! The Christian life cannot be lived without Christ. It takes living from your identity in Christ to walk out this Christian life. It takes His strength and ability flowing through us and a personal relationship with Him. He is our empowerment! He is our ability! He is our Joy! He is our strength! He is our hope! He is our everything!

Let These Bible Verses Encourage You

"Therefore if any man be in Christ, he is a new creature: old things are passed away; behold, all things are become new." *2 Corinthians 5:17*

"I am crucified with Christ: nevertheless I live; yet not I, but Christ liveth in me: and the life which I now live in the flesh I live by the faith of the Son of God, who loved me, and gave himself for me." *Galatians 2:20*

"Remember ye not the former things, neither consider the things of old. Behold, I will do a new thing; now it shall spring forth; shall ye not know it? I will even make a way in the wilderness, and rivers in the desert." Isaiah 43:18-19

"Therefore if any man be in Christ, he is a new creature: old things are passed away; behold, all things are become new.And all things are of God, who hath reconciled us to himself by Jesus Christ, and hath given to us the ministry of reconciliation;To wit, that God was in Christ, reconciling the world unto himself, not imputing their trespasses unto them; and hath committed unto us the word of reconciliation.For he hath made him to be sin for us, who knew no sin; that we might be made the righteousness of God in him."
2 Corinthians 5:17-21

"Lie not one to another, seeing that ye have put off the old man with his deeds; And have put on the new man, which is renewed in knowledge after the image of him that created him." Colossians 3:9-10

"If ye then be risen with Christ, seek those things which are above, where Christ sitteth on the right hand of God. Set your affection on things above, not on things on the earth.For ye are dead, and your life is hid with Christ in God. When Christ, who is our life, shall appear, then shall ye also appear with him in glory." Colossians 3:1-4

"For we are his workmanship, created in Christ Jesus unto good works, which God hath before ordained that we should walk in them." Ephesians 2:10

"What shall we say then? Shall we continue in sin, that grace may abound? God forbid. How shall we, that are dead to sin, live any longer therein? Know ye not, that so many of us as were baptized into Jesus Christ were baptized into his death? Therefore we are buried with him by baptism into death: that like as Christ was raised up from the dead by the glory of the Father, even so we also should walk in newness of life.For if we have been planted together in the likeness of his death, we

shall be also in the likeness of his resurrection: Knowing this, that our old man is crucified with him, that the body of sin might be destroyed, that henceforth we should not serve sin. For he that is dead is freed from sin. Now if we be dead with Christ, we believe that we shall also live with him: Knowing that Christ being raised from the dead dieth no more; death hath no more dominion over him. For in that he died, he died unto sin once: but in that he liveth, he liveth unto God. Likewise reckon ye also yourselves to be dead indeed unto sin, but alive unto God through Jesus Christ our Lord. Let not sin therefore reign in your mortal body, that ye should obey it in the lusts thereof. Neither yield ye your members as instruments of unrighteousness unto sin: but yield yourselves unto God, as those that are alive from the dead, and your members as instruments of righteousness unto God. For sin shall not have dominion over you: for ye are not under the law, but under grace. What then? shall we sin, because we are not under the law, but under grace? God forbid. Know ye not, that to whom ye yield yourselves servants to obey, his servants ye are to whom ye obey; whether of sin unto death, or of obedience unto righteousness? But God be thanked, that ye were the servants of sin, but ye have obeyed from the heart that form of doctrine which was delivered you.Being then made free from sin, ye became the servants of righteousnessI speak after the manner of men because of the infirmity of your flesh: for as ye have yielded your members servants to uncleanness and to iniquity unto iniquity; even so now yield your members servants to righteousness unto holiness. For when ye were the servants of sin, ye were free from righteousness.What fruit had ye then in those things whereof ye are now ashamed? for the end of those things is death. But now being made free from sin, and become servants to God, ye have your fruit unto holiness, and the end everlasting life. For the wages of sin is death; but the gift of God is eternal life through Jesus Christ our Lord."
Romans 6:1-23

"By which he has granted to us his precious and very great promises, so that through them you may become partakers of the divine nature, having escaped from the corruption that is in the world because of sinful desire." 2 Peter 1:4

"To put off your old self, which belongs to your former manner of life and is corrupt through deceitful desires, and to be renewed in the spirit of your minds, and to put on the new self, created after the likeness of God in true righteousness and holiness." Ephesians 4:22-24

"And we all, with unveiled face, beholding the glory of the Lord, are being transformed into the same image from one degree of glory to another. For this comes from the Lord who is the Spirit." 2 Corinthians 3:18

"For God so loved the world, that he gave his only begotten Son, that whosoever believeth in him should not perish, but have everlasting life.For God sent not his Son into the world to condemn the world; but that the world through him might be saved." John 3:16-17

"Jesus answered and said unto him, Verily, verily, I say unto thee, Except a man be born again, he cannot see the kingdom of God." John 3:3

"For our citizenship is in heaven, from which we also eagerly wait for the Savior, the Lord Jesus Christ."
Philipians 3:20

CHAPTER 11

KNOW HIM AND MAKE HIM KNOWN

You were created to know God and to make Him known. You were created to build a relationship with God and to get to know Him in a personal way. God desires to walk with you and talk with you. He desires to build with you and for you to build with Him. God is our heavenly Father and we are His children in Christ Jesus. God as our Heavenly Father desires to build a personal relationship with us the same way a natural Father desires to build a personal relationship with his son.

The reality is for a relationship to happen on any level it takes a mutual desire to get to know each other on both ends. God desires that we know Him in a personal way and there is nothing greater than a personal relationship with God. In order for that to happen though, it requires us to reach out to Him. It takes us opening our hearts to Him and continually seeking Him. The Bible says, "seek and you shall find, ask and you shall receive, knock and the door shall open." For us to get to know God, we must willingly step out in faith to seek Him.

It is an honor, privilege, and pleasure to get to know Him. It is an exciting and divine opportunity that was made available to humanity because of the life of Christ, blood of Christ, death of Christ, and the resurrection of Christ. A personal relationship with God is not something that we should take lightly. it is something that we are to be radically grateful for. It is something that should be embraced with faith, hope, love, celebration, respect, and honor.

Getting to know God in a personal way is exciting. Getting to know Him is empowering, fulfilling, life-changing, and transforming. Getting to know Him is eternally impacting. The only thing that could fill the void and emptiness on the inside of a human being to overflow is an ongoing growing personal relationship with God.

I would not be who I am today or where I am today without a personal relationship with God. Out of a personal relationship with God, you can continually experience God's everlasting joy, a peace from God that surpasses human reasoning, and divine hope that only comes from the Lord Jesus Christ. An ongoing growing personal relationship with God puts you in a place where you are unstoppable, unshakable, and untouchable by the devil.

How do you build a personal relationship with God? It is very simple…You build a relationship with God by faith. You build a relationship with God by allowing His love for you to be the driving force of your life. You build a relationship with God through prayer, talking to Him. You build a relationship with God by reading His word. You build a relationship with God by worshiping Him in spirit and in truth. You build a personal relationship with God by renewing your mind with the truth of God's word declared in faith out of your mouth. You build a relationship with God by living out of your identity in Christ Jesus. You build a personal relationship with God by living a life of repentance of sins and faith in Jesus Christ.

You build a relationship with God by loving God with all of your heart, all your soul, all of your mind, and loving your neighbor as you love yourself. You build a relationship with God by giving Him your best and living for Him, joyfully offering yourself as a living sacrifice. As you do that, He will continually reveal Himself to you. He will give you insight and show you things as His Holy Spirit enlightens you.

The more you build a relationship with God and get to know Him, the more clear His voice will become.

You will also continue to get better at yielding to His inward promptings and inclinations. As your personal relationship with Him continues to grow, you will learn how to let Him direct you in everything you do, in all the decisions you make, big or small.

It is vital for you to seek God in the morning right when you get up. It is key for you to have a time of prayer, worship, and Bible reading right when you wake up. Even if you have to wake up earlier than normal, do what you have to do to have time with God. Take time in the morning to plead the blood of Jesus and to declare the word of God over your life. Do it over your family and over your day, house, car, over every situation and circumstance. Decree and declare protection over your life, in the name of Jesus. Rebuke the defeated devil in the name of Jesus. Ask God's Holy Spirit to guide and direct you.

Take authority in Christ and use the weaponry God gave you. When you take time to seek God in the morning, you set the pace and tone for your day. By taking time to seek God before your day starts when you wake up, you clothe yourself in His love, peace, protection, faith, and hope before you leave your house. Check out the chapter on prayer and authority in Christ for deeper revelation on the truths in this paragraph.

Building a relationship with God is something we should be doing throughout the day. I understand we live in a physical world where people have jobs and different responsibilities. However, a personal relationship with God will only help you be more effective in your everyday life. A real personal relationship with God by grace through faith in Jesus

Christ through His Holy Spirit will only be a blessing to you in all areas of your life.

Everything you do in this life should be out of your relationship with God. Everything we do, we do it unto the Lord. Everything we do, we do it for the glory of God. Everything we do, we are to do it in excellence. After all, we are representing God's Kingdom! Remember we are the body of Christ, we are a people of faith. We are not a people of doubt and unbelief. We are believers, not doubters; our confidence is in God. Our trust is in the Lord Jesus Christ.

A personal relationship with God can only be built in faith. Like I said at the beginning of this chapter, we get to know Him by faith. We pray in faith, read the Bible in faith, worship Him in faith, renew our minds by declaring His words in faith, and share the Gospel of Jesus Christ in faith. The Christian life is one that is lived out by faith.

We live with divine confidence in God believing and knowing that when we worship Him, He inhabits our worship. When we talk to Him and we pray He hears us. We listen to His voice in faith believing we can hear Him. We read the Bible in faith believing He is going to reveal things to us. We confess His word and words of faith believing that the atmosphere is shifting and things are changing. A personal relationship with God is built by grace through faith, and the fuel is the love of God.

God does not just desire that we get to know Him in a personal way. God also desires that we make Him *known*. God desires that out of our relationship with Him we spread the message of His Son Jesus

Christ to this hurting world. He desires that we make Him known by allowing His glory to shine through the motives of our hearts, the thoughts that we think, the words that we speak, and the actions that we make. He desires that we make Him known by joyfully living a life that glorifies Him.

He desires that we make Him known by preaching, teaching, living, and demonstrating the glorious Gospel of Jesus Christ. He desires that we make Him known by telling people about the life of Christ, the blood of Christ, the death of Christ, and the resurrection of Christ. He wants us to share with others the truth of how Jesus Christ defeated the devil and his demons, sin, death, hell, and the grave through His Life, death, bloodshed, and resurrection.

God desires that we make Him known by reaching out to people and praying with them. He wants us to encourage them and share our Jesus testimony with them. God desires that we make Him known by living a life of love, faith, hope, and forgiveness. He wants us to make Him known by allowing life to come out of our mouths and not death. By being the hands and feet of Jesus, a tangible expression of God's heart on the earth, we represent and make Him known. We also must see people how God sees them, through the lens of God's love that was demonstrated and made available through Jesus.

God desires that we make Him known by refraining from gossip. He desires that we make Him known by living a life of character, integrity, and kindness. God desires that we make Him known by living a life of compassion, tangibly demonstrating the message of God's grace in Christ Jesus. God desires that we get to know Him and that we make Him known. Every single person has a divine plan and purpose from God. His ultimate plan is for us to build a personal relationship with Him and to grow His kingdom by making Him known through the preaching, teaching, living, and demonstrating of the glorious Gospel of Jesus Christ.

It may look a little different for every individual, but no matter what someone is called to do, they are called to build a personal relationship with God and to advance His kingdom on the earth, through the Gospel of Jesus Christ. God desires that we enjoy the journey and take one step at a time. He wants us to embrace one moment at a time and fulfill the call of God on our lives with gratitude. Life with Jesus Christ is an adventure of faith.

Get to know Him and make Him known. In the next chapters, I will continue to share God-inspired revelation on different Biblical truths. Get ready for your roots to grow deeper in things of God. Get excited as a stronger Kingdom of God Biblical foundation is laid. This will be a foundation for you to build on that empowers you to live a life that glorifies God, advances His kingdom on the earth, and makes an eternal impact on this generation for Jesus. Get excited, stay hungry, teachable, and full of faith as you go through the next chapters.

Let These Bible Verses Encourage You

"And he answering said, Thou shalt love the Lord thy God with all thy heart, and with all thy soul, and with all thy strength, and with all thy mind; and thy neighbor as thyself."
Luke 10:27

"But grow in grace, and in the knowledge of our Lord and Savior Jesus Christ. To him be glory both now and forever. Amen." 2 Peter 3:18

"That I may know him, and the power of his resurrection, and the fellowship of his sufferings, being made conformable unto his death." Philipians 3:10

*"And this is life eternal, that they might know thee the only true God, and Jesus Christ, whom thou hast sent."
John 17:3*

*"Thy word is a lamp unto my feet, and a light unto my path."
Psalms 118:105*

"Whosoever abideth in him sinneth not: whosoever   sinneth hath not seen him, neither known him." 1 John 3:6

"And be not conformed to this world: but be ye transformed by the renewing of your mind, that ye may prove what is that good, and acceptable, and perfect, will of God." Romans 12:2

*"For I know the thoughts that I think toward you, saith the LORD, thoughts of peace, and not of evil, to give you an expected end."
Jeremiah 29:11*

"And he said unto them, Go ye into all the world, and preach the gospel to every creature." Mark 16:15

"For I am not ashamed of the gospel of Christ: for it is the power of God unto salvation to every one that believeth; to the Jew first, and also to the Greek." Romans 1:16

"Preach the word; be instant in season, out of season; reprove, rebuke, exhort with all long suffering and doctrine." 2 Timothy 4:2

"But ye shall receive power, after that the Holy Ghost is come upon you: and ye shall be witnesses unto me both in Jerusalem, and in all Judaea, and in Samaria, and unto the uttermost part of the earth." Acts 1:8

"For ye are all the children of God by faith in Christ Jesus." Galatians 3:26

"Heal the sick, cleanse the lepers, raise the dead, cast out devils: freely ye have received, freely give." Mathew 10:8

"And this gospel of the kingdom shall be preached in all the world for a witness unto all nations; and then shall the end come." Matthew 24:14

"Go ye therefore, and teach all nations, baptizing them in the name of the Father, and of the Son, and of the Holy Ghost." Matthew 28:19

"From that time Jesus began to preach, and to say,Repent: for the kingdom of heaven is at hand." Matthew 4:17

"And Jesus went about all Galilee, teaching in their synagogues, and preaching the gospel of the kingdom, and healing all manner of sickness and all manner of disease among the people." Matthew 4:23

"But seek ye first the kingdom of God, and his righteousness; and all these things shall be added unto you." Matthew 6:33

"For whosoever shall call upon the name of the Lord shall be saved." Romans 10:13

"I appeal to you therefore, brothers, by the mercies of God, to present your bodies as a living sacrifice, holy and acceptable to God, which is your spiritual worship." Romans 12:1

"For God so loved the world, that he gave his only begotten Son, that whosoever believeth in him should not perish, but have everlasting life." John 3:16

CHAPTER 12

THE POWER OF THE BIBLE, WORSHIP, AND PRAYER.

THE POWER OF THE BIBLE

The Bible is tangible and alive. The Bible is an unshakable foundation. The Bible is God-inspired, the Bible is God-breathed, the Bible is supernatural. The

Bible is God's love letter to the human race. The Bible is beautiful, the Bible is amazing, the Bible is energizing. The Bible is our divine manual for life. Operating in Biblical principles out of a relationship with God by grace through faith in Jesus, will always set you up for divine success. The Bible is not a random piece of literature; the Bible is supernatural God-given literature provided to us by God Himself. The Bible is food to eat, water to drink, and oxygen to breathe in. The Bible is a rock-solid foundation for you to build your life on so when the storms come it does not fall apart.

There is not a book greater than the Bible nor is there a book more exciting than the Bible. The Bible is supernaturally exciting, eternal; the Bible is the Word of God. When you read the Bible in expectation and in faith believing that God is going to reveal something to you, He always does. He is a God that is always revealing Himself when we read His word. As we seek Him and experience Him through reading His Word, He always gives us divine insight and understanding.

There is no greater privilege than getting to know God on a personal basis. Jesus Christ made a personal relationship with God possible through His life, death, bloodshed, and resurrection. One way of getting to know Him is by reading the Bible. You must read it from the position of who you are in Christ. The Bible is God's words, thoughts, and ideas. By reading it we can learn how He moves, how He flows, and how He operates. God does not want us to just read the Bible to read it, but He desires that we read it to eat it, out of a relationship with Him. God desires that we embrace the Bible, celebrate, enjoy and respect it. He wants us to truly enjoy and love His Word. God desires that we glorify, worship, and praise Him in Spirit and in truth for the Bible. He desires that we thank Him for the Bible and that we are grateful for the Bible.

There is not a book that is more powerful than the Bible on this planet. There is no other book that is more interesting than the Bible. There are more Bibles printed on earth than any other book. There is eternal, Holy Spirit revelation knowledge made available to you as you read the Bible. Revelation knowledge from God is simply divine understanding and insight given from Him when we read the Bible. The Bible has radically changed my life, supernaturally increased my wisdom, knowledge, and understanding, because it comes from God Himself.

God desires that His Word be the foundation on which you build your life on. Building your life on His word and building your life on His truth will cause you to be unstoppable for His glory. God desires that you value His word and He desires that you never take His Word lightly. God desires that we live according to His truth and that we take action on what He says. God desires that we are doers of His Word and not just hearers only. By taking action on what He says, we will see the Bible manifest in our own lives. We will produce God results, live with the fruits of the Holy Spirit, operate in His gifts, and be effective for His Kingdom.

If you do not own a Bible, find a way to get one. Contact our ministry so we can find a way to get you a Bible. Physical Bibles can be found at Christian bookstores or anywhere that books are sold. You can download a digital Bible in the app store on your phone. A good Bible app to download is the "YouVersion" Bible app, and it is free to download.

Even if you download a digital Bible, you should have a physical Bible. There is just something about having a physical Bible in your hands. Once you get your Bible, I encourage you to read it, underline different verses that speak to you, highlight things that God shows you. Buy a journal or notebook so you can write notes and document different things that God speaks to you about.

I encourage you to find times throughout your day to build a personal relationship with God through reading the Bible. The Bible is divided into two major sections, the Old and New testament. The best Book for you to start off reading is the book of John in the New Testament. There are many ways to read the Bible and enjoy the Bible. You can read your Bible from Genesis to Revelation. You can read it by focusing on specific topics or themes. You can read it by meditating on specific paragraphs or verses. I encourage you to start out with the New Testament. Read from Matthew to Revelation and then journey through Genesis to Revelation. What you will realize is that the Bible is one big love letter written to you by God.

You will begin to notice that everything in the Bible points to Jesus Christ, the Savior of humanity who made redemption available through His life, death, bloodshed, and resurrection. God desires that as we read the Bible, we read it being fully conscious of who we are in Christ Jesus. He wants us to be aware of the identity that we received when we repented of our sins and believed in Jesus Christ. He wants us to know that we are loved, pursued, embraced, and desired by God. That is why He sent His Son Jesus Christ to the earth. He sent Jesus to save us, heal us, restore us, reconcile us, redeem us, love us, and the beautiful God-given list continues. The Bible is food for your spirit and water that washes your soul. The Bible is a foundation that cannot be shaken.

God knew the Bible was going to be written before the foundations of the world. He knew it was going to be released to the nations of the world. He knew it would be given to the people of the earth to support, encourage, uplift, correct, exhort, build up, heal, restore, and inspire people to love and worship Him. He knew this would empower humanity to share the good news of Jesus Christ. As you read the Bible, read it as if you were in the pages. Read it as if you were there at the moment. Read it believing that God is going to give you impartations from His Holy Spirit. The Bible is a blessing, the Bible is a miracle, and the Bible alive.

There are many good resources on the Bible. This section of the Bible that you just read is simply to encourage you on the power of the Bible. I love my Bible and I read it every day. The Bible forever impacted my life and continues to daily impact my life. I encourage you to add reading the Bible and your personal devotions with the Lord right when you wake up. Do not allow anything to stop you from reading the Bible. It is a gift from God directly to you. God is always speaking to us and the number one way he does so is through His Word, the Bible.

Praise God for the Bible! The next section of this God-given Chapter is on the power of PRAISE AND WORSHIP! Get ready because you are going to be blessed!

Let These Bible Verses Encourage You

"For the word of God is quick, and powerful, and sharper than any two edged sword, piercing even to the dividing asunder of soul and spirit, and of the joints and marrow, and is a discerner of the thoughts and intents of the heart."
Hebrews 4:12

"All scripture is given by inspiration of God, and is profitable for doctrine, for reproof, for correction, for instruction in righteousness: That the man of God may be perfect, thoroughly furnished unto all good works."
2 Timothy 3:16-17

"Thy word is a lamp unto my feet, and a light unto my path."
Psalm 119:105

"This Book of the Law shall not depart from your mouth, but you shall meditate on it day and night, so that you may be careful to do according to all that is written in it. For then you will make your way prosperous, and then you will have good success."
2 Timothy 3:16-17

*"The grass withereth, the flower fadeth:
but the word of our God shall stand for ever."*
Isaiah 40:8

"But he said, Yea rather, blessed are they that hear the word of God, and keep it."
Luke 11:28

THE POWER OF PRAISE AND WORSHIP

Praise and worship unto God is what we give Him because of who He is. He is the Creator of the earth, the moon, and the stars. He is the creator of the Universe. He created the human race and He is the Creator of all the animals, different kinds of fruits, and the ocean. Praise and worship unto God is something that should flow freely out of our relationship with God. God desires that we desire to worship and praise Him. We praise and worship Him not only because of who He is, but also because of what He has done. We praise and worship Him because He sent Jesus Christ to redeem humanity. Without Jesus Christ, we as God's creation would never be able to worship God in spirit and in truth. The blood of Jesus Christ and what He made available at the cross through His life, death, bloodshed, and resurrection, is the only reason we can even worship God in spirit and in truth.

Worship and praise unto God are not just the songs that we sing, even though in this chapter we mainly focus on the singing side of worship and praise. Worship and praise unto God also includes the motives of our hearts, the thoughts that we think, the words that we speak, and the actions that we make. Praise and worship unto God is the way we treat people and how we handle situations. Of course, praise and worship unto God does flow through songs but it is not the only way that God is glorified. He desires that our lives glorify Him. Living a life of faith, hope, love, and forgiveness is worship unto God. Singing songs that glorify Him is worship unto Him. Praise and worship unto God is a heart posture, a mindset, and it is a lifestyle. God called us to be worshipers...

There is power in praise and worship unto God. The Bible says in John 4:23-24 that there is a generation of Spirit and Truth worshipers rising up. There is a group of people who will worship God in Spirit and in Truth. When you repented of your sins, confessed your sins to God, and put your faith in Jesus Christ as your Lord and Savior, you received a regenerated spirit and you became one with Christ. You became a brand new creation in Christ Jesus. God desires that we worship Him from that place, the beautiful glorious truth of you being a born-again spirit in Christ Jesus. He desires that we worship Him from a place of knowing the divine truth of who He is. God desires that you cast all of your cares on Him and that you worship Him from that place. He wants you to sing songs of adoration and exultation unto Him.

He loves it when you sing to Him while worshiping and praising Him. An example would be singing songs that have phrases like, "Hallelujah, God I praise you, God I worship you. I lift you up, true living God. You are my everything." Sing songs like, "I sing praises unto you, King Jesus Christ." The Bible says the angels surround the throne of God singing out, "Holy Holy Holy is the Lord God Almighty." The Bible says that there is worship unto Him taking place around His throne twenty-four-seven. God loves to be worshiped. He loves to be praised and exalted. It is as simple as singing unto Him from your born-again spirit in Christ, from that place of being in Him. He wants you to worship Him out of the truth of who He is, the truth of who you are in Him, and the truth of His word. It is as simple as singing to Him from that place. Sing phrases like, "Holy Holy Holy, is the Lord God Almighty, who was and is and is to come." When you sing to God, He inhabits your praises unto Him.

When you exalt the true living God, He receives pleasure. Furthermore, as you worship Him, the atmosphere shifts and something takes place in the spirit realm. There is a shift in the spirit realm as the peace of Heaven and peace of God that surpasses all understanding begins to manifest around you and within you. When you worship God the joy of heaven and the joy of God begins to manifest around you and begins to manifest in you. When you worship God in spirit and truth, even if just for five minutes, you will notice something change. As you worship Him, He moves on your behalf and causes things to take place. As you go deeper into worshiping God, you will notice a clarity beginning to consume you. Your eyes and ears will be opened up to what God is saying. Oftentimes people suffer from depression, anxiety, jealousy, or other tormenting emotions because their mouth is silent. Furthermore, they may also be meditating on the lies of the devil. When you combine meditation of the devil's lies, with a closed mouth, it sets the person up for demonic torment. That is one of the devil's demonic equations for destruction.

When somebody keeps their mouth closed and meditates on the devil's lies, or they only speak words of death, destruction begins to take place in that person's mind. This will begin to affect their emotions, physical body or health, and their overall life. A lot of people are suffering because they have yet to catch a revelation of the powerful, glorious, beautiful truth of worshiping God in spirit and in truth. There needs to be a personal revelation of worshiping God every day, Monday through Sunday, and living a life of worship unto God.

It is key to understand when it comes to praising and worshiping God, that it is not about having the best voice or the best tone. It is all about your heart posture, and doing it from your born-again spirit which is one with Christ. Worship out of the truth of God's word, who you are in Christ, and the divine truth of who He is, the true living God. Cast your cares on Him and sing from that place as you exalt Him. As you worship God from that place of faith believing that God is inhabiting your praise and worship unto Him, you will notice that the tormenting emotions of depression, anxiety, and fear will disappear. Those demonic destructive thoughts will disappear. Worshiping God is one way that your mind is renewed.

When you worship God, the emotions of Heaven begin to manifest. Those emotions include joy, peace, patience, gladness, hope, etc. He gives you clarity and He gives you direction. God never created us to only worship Him just for thirty minutes on a Sunday. God desires that we worship Him *daily*, that we exalt Him *daily*. He desires that we live from that place, understanding that we were made to worship Him. God desires that we live a life that is fueled by a revelation of His love for us, proven through Jesus. God Desires that we live this life on earth from that place of His love. When you put your faith in Jesus Christ, you were born of God's love, born of His incorruptible seed, and of His spirit. You were born of God, the true living God. Not just that but the Bible says that His love was shed abroad in our hearts. God desires that you live and worship Him from that place. I want to encourage you to never be silent again. Choose to joyfully live a life of spirit and truth worship and praise unto the TRUE LIVING GOD. Worshiping Him changes everything...

I decree and declare in the name of Jesus Christ from this moment on, that an impartation from the Holy Spirit is taking place in your life. From here on out, you are going to live a life that worships God in spirit and in truth. You are going to live a life of worship unto God, singing to Him and worshiping Him daily. You will begin to notice a greater peace and joy that comes from God as Heaven invades your life in ways you never thought or imagined. From this moment, you will begin to experience clarity and direction in ways you never thought or imagined from God's Holy Spirit as you live a life of worship unto Him.

I want to encourage you that one of the number one ways that you worship God is by singing to Him out of your mouth and exalting Him. Singing songs of worship, praise, exaltation, and adoration unto Him are some ways to do so. As I said at the beginning of this chapter, God also desires that we understand that worship is not just the songs that we sing but also the motives of our hearts, the thoughts that we think, the words that we speak, the actions that we make, and the life that we live. The Apostle Paul said, "Don't you know that you are the temple of the Holy Spirit, therefore honor God with your bodies." God desires that we worship Him, and yes that we sing to Him; but He also wants us to recognize that He is also worshiped through the motives of our hearts. When the motive of our heart is to glorify God and to do everything for Him, He is worshiped. He wants our motives to line up with His word and for us to ultimately live a life that is in line with His word.

God is worshiped when you filter your thought life with His word, managing the thoughts that you think and renewing your mind with the word of God. When you notice a thought that should not be in your mind, that does not glorify God, fill your mouth with the word of God. The truth of His word spoken or sang through your mouth causes your mind to be renewed. This enables you to feel His presence. God desires that you speak life, that you speak words that glorify Him, and that you speak faith.

God is worshiped with the words of your mouth, words that line up with His word. God is worshiped when you share the message of Jesus Christ, when you share your testimony of how you encountered Jesus Christ and how He transformed your life. That is all a form of worship unto Him. When you pray with people, speak to others about the goodness of His grace, mercy, and His love, God is honored. God is worshiped when we decide to manifest His kingdom by preaching, teaching, living, and demonstrating the glorious Gospel of Jesus Christ.

Your life is so valuable to God and He truly loves you so much. He has placed things in you that this world needs. We are each a vital part of God's Kingdom; we are the body of Christ. I believe that God is going to continue to use your life as a divine testimony of His grace and as a witness and demonstration of His power. We are in this together, Jesus Christ is coming soon. Be who God has called *you* to be, do what God has called *you* to do. Hallelujah to the Most High GOD! There is power in worshiping and praising God in spirit and in truth.

You can worship God in your house, in the car, inside or outside of a building; you can worship and praise Him anywhere. You can praise and worship Him with a song or with instruments. I want to encourage you to take time right when you wake up in the morning to worship God and praise Him every single day. Have a moment every morning where you sing to Him and spend time with Him through prayer, talking to Him. Spend time with Him through reading the Bible, His written word. Take the time to declare and decree His word over your day. Set the tone for your day by seeking Him *first*. Do life with Him and include Him in your decisions. Make praise and worship unto Him part of your daily life.

Praise and worship Him for who He is and for all the spiritual blessings (redemption package, identity in Christ, authority in Christ) that He made available to you through the life, death, bloodshed, and resurrection of Jesus Christ. Praise and worship Him for all of the physical blessings He has given you such as oxygen in your lungs, your eyes, ears, body, overall health, food, your house, car, etc. Praise and worship Him for all that He has done, all that He is doing, and all that He is going to do in the future. Praise and worship Him for protection and answered prayers. Praise Him in faith, rejoicing as if all your prayers have already been answered. We have so many reasons to praise and worship Him. The number one reason you praise, worship and thank Him is because He is worthy of all the honor and glory. He is the Most High GOD, the only true living GOD, the faithful GOD, the Almighty GOD. He is the GREAT I AM.

Praise Him for the past, praise Him for the now, praise Him for the future. In Christ Jesus the past, present, and future is bright!

Let These Bible Verses Encourage You

"I will bless the Lord at all times: his praise shall continually be in my mouth. My soul shall make her boast in the Lord: the humble shall hear thereof, and be glad. O magnify the Lord with me, and let us exalt his name together." Psalms 34

"God is a Spirit: and they that worship him must worship him in spirit and in truth."
John 4:24

"Let my mouth be filled with thy praise
and with thy honour all the day." Psalm 71:8

"O Lord, thou art my God;
I will exalt thee, I will praise thy name;
for thou hast done wonderful things;
thy counsels of old are faithfulness and truth."
Isaiah 25:1

"In God I will praise his word,
in God I have put my trust;
I will not fear what flesh can do unto me."
Psalm 56:4

THE POWER OF PRAYER.

There is supernatural power in prayer. I think about how my mom prayed for me when I looked impossible. I was running away from God, rejecting Him, and on the path of destruction. Thank God my mom and dad were praying over me, speaking God's word over me, and also standing in agreement with other people for me. Even though my mother's prayers were not answered immediately, her prayer for me was eventually answered.

You see, my mom and dad prayed from a place of faith, and a place of righteousness in Christ. They prayed from a place of celebration, knowing that God was and is faithful. My parents prayed with expectation, knowing that God was going to answer their prayer. They prayed with joy as if their prayer was already answered. They prayed in the name of Jesus. My parents prayed from a position of trusting and putting their confidence in God.

A simple way to explain prayer is a "conversation with God." Furthermore, there is also a side of prayer where we *listen*. There are different kinds of prayers according to the Bible, which I will be going over in this chapter. I encourage you to use a prayer journal so when you are having a time of prayer and God begins to speak to you, you can write down what He is telling you. Please know that if God tells you something it is because there is a supernatural purpose behind it. It is such a joy to know that because of Jesus, we can have a personal relationship with the true living God through His Holy Spirit. It is such a joy to know that Christianity is not a religion, but rather a personal relationship with God by grace through faith in Jesus Christ, through God's Holy Spirit.

I believe God's grace and my parent's prayers are two main reasons why I accepted Jesus Christ as my Lord and Savior. I believe that is one of the reasons that I am living out God's plans and purposes for my life today. There is power in prayer. If you have loved ones that are running away from Jesus, I encourage you to pray for them. Do not give up on them but continue to intercede on the behalf of their lives. God will answer your prayers and you will see them get right with God by grace through faith in Jesus Christ. Praise God!

God desires that when we pray, we pray from a place of personal relationship, a place of heart intimacy with Him. He wants us to pray from a place of faith, expectation and joy from our hearts. He does not desire that we just say the same thing over and over as the pharisees did in the Bible. He does not want religious repetition with no relationship, no faith, no expectation, and no heart intimacy with Him. In Luke 11, we see

Jesus teaching on prayer and I encourage you to read that chapter. I recommend in your personal Bible study time that you grab a highlighter, pick a specific color, and highlight different verses on prayer. That will also aid you in your prayer life.

"One day Jesus was praying in a certain place. When He finished, one of His disciples said to him, 'Lord, teach us to pray, just as John taught his disciples.' He said to them, 'When you pray, say: Father, hallowed be your Name, your Kingdom come. Give us each day our daily bread. Forgive us our sins, for we also forgive everyone who sins against us. And lead us not into temptation.'" Luke 11:1-3

"Jesus said 'Pray, then, in this way: Our Father who is in Heaven, Hallowed be Your Name. Thy Kingdom come, thy will be done, on earth as it is in Heaven. Give us this day our daily bread. And forgive us our debts, as we also have forgiven our debtors. And do not lead us into temptation, but deliver us from evil. For Yours is the Kingdom and the power and the glory forever. Amen. For if you forgive others for their transgressions, your heavenly Father will also forgive you. But if you do not forgive others, then your Father will not forgive your transgressions.'" Mathew 6:9-14

Prayer is powerful and one thing that I have realized is that we cannot walk out what we have not prayed out. God desires that we pray things into existence. The same way my mother prayed my salvation into existence, is the same way the salvation of your loved ones can be prayed out and spoken into existence, in the name of Jesus. Just how I prayed out and spoke out all the things that the Lord has done through my life over these years by His grace, mercy, and love, is the same way you can pray and speak into existence God's plan for your life.

Prayer is another avenue in which we can commune with God, get to know Him, experience Him, build a relationship with Him, and receive revelation from Him. Remember prayer is not just speaking, but there is also a listening side to prayer. God desires that in our prayer times we also pray with listening ears. He wants us to listen to what He is saying on the inside of us. Always be ready to write down what He speaks to you, including the verses, encouragements, etc. Write it down in your prayer journal and remember that you have a personal relationship with Him. What a joy to know that through prayer, worship, and the bible we can build a personal relationship with the Maker of the Universe, THE TRUE LIVING GOD!

Sometimes you will end up in tears during times of prayer, not necessarily because you are sad but because of how comforting He is, how amazing He is, the power of His love and His presence. Sometimes you will laugh in times of prayer because of how amazing and loving, and His beautiful presence. In your times of prayer always be authentic, be yourself, and put your heart into it. Remember God is your Heavenly Father and you are His Child in Christ Jesus.

When we pray, God desires that we pray in the name of Jesus Christ. The Bible says that at the name of Jesus every knee has to bow. That means depression, anxiety, negativity, fear, sickness, whatever it is has to bow to the name of Jesus Christ. Jesus Christ is our mediator; He is the bridge that reconciled us back to God. As born-again new creations in Christ, we have the legal right to use the name of Jesus. We have the legal right and personal access to God.

The Bible says that at the name of Jesus defeated demons flee. We can drive out and cast out demons at the name of Jesus. The devil and his demons come to kill, steal and destroy but Christ Jesus came to give us life and give it to us more abundantly, according to John 10:10. We are able to drive out demons by using the name of Jesus Christ. We have supernatural authority in Christ Jesus. We have supernatural dominion in Christ Jesus. As I mentioned in earlier chapters, everything that Adam lost in the garden, Jesus restored at the cross.

God desires that we pray out of the position and identity that we have in Christ Jesus. We must understand that we have supernatural dominion in Christ Jesus and know that we are citizens of Heaven. We are in covenant with the true living God because of our faith in Jesus Christ. There is power in prayer!

Here Is A Basic List Of Different Ways You Can Pray

Prayer of Thanksgiving

Supplication

Intercessory Prayer

Corporate or Public Prayer

Closet or Private Prayer

Declaration

Decreeing

Listening

Prayer of Consecration

Prayer of Faith

Prayer in Tongues

Prayer is Conversation with God

Prayer of Adoration

Prayer of Confession

Prayer of Vows

Prayer of Quiet Reflection

Prayer for healing

Prayer for Deliverance and Help

Prayer of Salvation and Rededication

Prayer of Intercession

Prayer for Transformation

Prayer of Blessing

& the Beautiful list goes on...

I pray that this section on prayer blessed you and gives you something to work with, that you can build on and grow from. There is power in prayer! I pray in Jesus' name that you will have a powerful prayer life! Know that I believe in you and I am cheering you on. I pray that God's plans and purposes for your life will come to pass in Jesus' Name. I pray that you read these sections on prayer, the bible, and worship and that as you do you receive fresh impartation from the Holy Spirit. I pray you catch a fresh fire and passion for the things of God, a fire for the bible, worshiping God, praying, speaking the word of God, and sharing the good news of Jesus. Hallelujah to the Most High God!

I love to pray and I am grateful that God gave us the ability to do so. Prayer is a gift, joy, privilege, honor, and opportunity. Jesus prayed, the disciples and early church prayed, and God desires that *we* also pray. I encourage you to not only pray but to enjoy, celebrate and embrace it. There is power in prayer!

The next chapter is on the subject of the God given power of words and renewing your mind! Your words have the power of life and death. Your words are powerful and it is vital that every disciple of Jesus understands the power of their words. In the next chapter you will learn about this divine topic.

Let These Bible Verses Encourage You

"Continue in prayer, and watch in the same with thanksgiving."
Colossians 4:2

"Rejoicing in hope; patient in tribulation; continuing instant in prayer." Romans 12:12

"And all things, whatsoever ye shall ask in prayer, believing, ye shall receive."
Matthew 21:22

"Be careful for nothing; but in every thing by prayer and supplication with thanksgiving let your requests be made known unto God. And the peace of God, which passeth all understanding, shall keep your hearts and minds through Christ Jesus." Philippians 4:6-7

"For the eyes of the Lord are over the righteous, and his ears are open unto their prayers: but the face of the Lord is against them that do evil."
1 Peter 3:12

CHAPTER 13

THE POWER OF WORDS AND RENEWING YOUR MIND

God created the earth with His words. He created the universe with His words. He created the sun, moon, and stars with His words. God created the human race with His words, all the animals with His words, and all the different kinds of fruits with His words. God created all the different kinds of trees with His words, animals that can breathe underwater with His words, and ones that can fly with His words.

Today we see words everywhere. We see words in books, people speaking words on television, words on documents. There are words that we speak when we wake up and words that we speak throughout the day. There are words on bachelor's degree diplomas hanging on walls, words on shirts and billboards. The Bible is the living word of God. What a pleasure and privilege it is to have access to the Word of God.

God desires that we filter our mouth with His Word. He desires that life comes out of our mouth and that we declare His words out of our mouth. God desires that we refrain from speaking negativity and words of death. He wants us to have positive speech and speak words of life. He desires that we declare and decree His Word.

The Bible says the tongue is like a small rudder of a ship that directs your life. Your tongue is the steering wheel of your life. Wherever you are currently at in life, reality is you spoke yourself into that position. God desires that we have a filter on our mouth, our thought life, and the gateways to our soul. Your eyes, ears and mouth are all gateways. You must filter every gateway with the word of God and only tolerate the word of God to come out of your mouth. There is tremendous power in the word of God and there is power when you speak His word. Take scriptures in the Bible, personalize them, speak them over your life, family, situations, and circumstances. There are over seven hundred promises for the born-again, new creation, in-Christ believer in the Bible. Find those promises and those things that God said are yours. For example, take Psalm 91 and confess it, make it personal. The Bible is one big, divine, eternal legal document. God does not lie and He only speaks the truth. After all, He *is* the truth. He desires that we understand our legal rights in Christ Jesus and operate in them.

Guard your brain and thoughts. Filter what you think about. Do not tolerate thoughts of depression, anxiety, or negativity. There is no pain in heaven, no sadness in heaven, no anxiety in heaven, no stress in heaven, no negativity in heaven. If it is not in heaven, do not tolerate it in your mind. Never tolerate it in your words or your body either. If you notice a negative thought in your brain, you need to renew your mind immediately by declaring God's word over your life.

For example, if a thought like, "I am alone, I am not gifted, I am worthless," comes to your mind, you need to fight that thought by declaring the Word of God. Declare, "I am not alone! Christ is with me. God has given me gifts and talents!" Declare, "Because of Jesus Christ, I have eternal value and I have been purchased by the blood of Jesus." Do not just try to fight a thought with another thought; it does not work that way. Overcome that negative thought with the Word of God on your lips. Confessing God's word over your life forces your mind to be renewed and transformed by the power and the glory of God.

Only tolerate joy, peace, excitement, hope, love, and celebration from Heaven in your life. What do you think the United States Army would do if another nation launched a missile directed towards their nation? The moment they saw it on the radar they would shoot another missile that would destroy the one directed to them before it ever landed on United States territory. In the same way, when you notice satan trying to launch a missile in the form of a thought against you, you need to use your mouth to shoot a missile of life against that negative missile. Your mouth is essentially a nuclear cannon in between your nose and chin. Look at your thought life, your emotions, your body, and your home, as God's territory. When anything tries to come against it, be quick to use your mouth to cancel out and destroy any works of the enemy trying to come against you. Remember there is supernatural power in the name of Jesus Christ!

When you have a filter on your thought life you will easily be able to identify if thoughts are from God or satan. Thoughts originating from God will always line up with the Bible. Thoughts originating from satan will always be negative, destructive, evil, and not be in line with the Word. In order for you to be a fruit-producing Christian, it is key to have a Holy Spirit filter and radar on your thought life. The devil is the father of lies and he has been doing it for a long time. He knows how to "press people's buttons," so to speak, and how to get them off course. It is vital that you have a Holy Spirit radar on your thought life. When the defeated devil tries to put a thought in your brain to make you worried, afraid, intimidated, jealous, or anxious, you need to quickly say, "No devil! Not today, not ever!" Combat the devil with a verse from the Bible, spoken from your mouth and with faith. Speak God's Word concerning what the devil was trying to get you to believe. I want to encourage you that there are many ways you can renew your mind. One of the most effective ways is the moment the devil presents you with a lie, you present him with *truth* to destroy that lie. Confess the truth of

God's Word at the name of Jesus and you will notice that negative thoughts evaporate. Another way that you can renew your mind is by worshiping God. Demons hate worship unto God. When you worship Him in Spirit and in truth, thoughts that are not of God evaporate.

The lies of the devil in your thought life evaporate from your mind when you pray in your known tongue (English or whatever language you speak), or in tongues Read Acts 2 to learn more about speaking in tongues. Satan's negative thoughts evaporate from your mind when you renew your mind with the spoken word of God. Be militant about renewing your mind. Remain serious about guarding your thought life. Stay focused on Jesus, focused on what He has called you to do and His plan for your life, focused on what you have to do for the day. Be grateful, love-rooted, and faith-rooted in the purpose that God has for you. Living the victorious life in Christ is directly connected to controlling your thought life the way God biblically desires you to control it. God has given you all of the weaponry you need to live the overcoming life in Christ Jesus. He wants you to only tolerate Heaven in your thoughts, Heaven in your emotions, Heaven in your body, Heaven in your words, and Heaven in your actions. God desires that you cultivate a life of Heaven on earth by living a life of communion with Him, a life of worship unto Him, a life of prayer, adoration, and a life of His Word.

In the teaching chapters of this book, you will notice that all of them supernaturally connect together. As you read this entire book, there is an impartation from the Holy Spirit that will take place that is going to be a blessing to you. There is going to be a kingdom mindset that you will grab ahold of that will radically impact your life. This book is different than a lot of books and I believe that as you read through it, you will receive a rock-solid foundation in basic Biblical truths. This will enable you to be effective for Him. I ultimately believe this book will help you strengthen your relationship with God!

We are living in exciting days. We are living in the last days. I believe Jesus Christ is getting ready to crack the sky and the body of Christ is going to be raptured. God desires that we as the body of Christ stir up passion for what He is about. He wants us to grow in passion for the great commission, what He has called us to do, and He who He has called us to be. In these last days, the body of Christ cannot be living in unforgiveness, gossip, slander, immorality, pornography, jealousy, division, sin, etc. If we are going to reach the lost, we need to stand out by living a pure life in Christ. We need to have pure motives, pure thoughts, pure words, pure actions, rooted out of our personal relationship with God. If we are going to stand out, we need to avoid the appearance of evil. Whether it be in our motives, thoughts, words, or actions, we must look different from the world.

God desires that we are rooted in Him and that we represent His kingdom with excellence. When people look at us they should see Jesus. When people look at us they should see someone pure in Christ. When people look at us they see someone Holy in Christ. When should reflect the love of God, tell the truth, live lives of integrity with a heart after God. Please note this does not mean that you are going to be perfect in all areas of your life. This just means that you will live for God with all that you are and all that He has given to you in spirit and in truth, for His glory. If you fall, just get back up, repent of your sins quickly and keep moving by faith in Jesus. Keep living a life that glorifies God in all areas of your life. We are the army of God. We are the body of Christ, the hands and feet of Jesus. We are a tangible expression of God's heart on the earth.

Remember to keep your mind renewed with the truth of the Word of God, using the weaponry God gave you. This weaponry includes prayer, worship, reading and speaking the Word in faith, the prayer of agreement, casting demons out at the name of Jesus, gratitude, and walking in love. Allowing the Holy Spirit to direct your life, living according to the truth of God's Word, your new creation in-Christ identity, and using the authority He gave you, are also examples of using your weaponry. Choose to forgive by faith, live in the fruits of the Holy Spirit, live a life of faith, and choose to live a life that glorifies God. God has given us everything that we need to live the overcoming victorious life in Christ Jesus. He has equipped us with all the weaponry we need to live a Holy Spirit fruit-producing life, filled with peace, joy, and hope. God has given us everything that we need to freely make an eternal impact on this hurting dark world through preaching, teaching, living, and demonstrating the glorious Gospel of Jesus Christ.

Let These Bible Verses Encourage You

"I beseech you therefore, brethren, by the mercies of God, that ye present your bodies a living sacrifice, holy, acceptable unto God, which is your reasonable service. And be not conformed to this world: but be ye transformed by the renewing of your mind, that ye may

prove what is that good, and acceptable, and perfect, will of God."
Romans 12:1-2

"And be renewed in the spirit of your mind."
Ephesians 4:23

"Finally, brethren, whatsoever things are true, whatsoever things are honest, whatsoever things are just, whatsoever things are pure, whatsoever things are lovely, whatsoever things are of good report; if there be any virtue, and if there be any praise, think on these things."
Philipians 4:8

"Death and life are in the power of the tongue: and they that love it shall eat the fruit thereof."
Proverbs 18:21

"For by thy words thou shalt be justified, and by thy words thou shalt be condemned."
Matthew 12:37

"Pleasant words are as an honeycomb, sweet to the soul, and health to the bones." Proverbs 16:24

"Thou wilt keep him in perfect peace, whose mind is stayed on thee: because he trusteth in thee." Isaiah 26:3

CHAPTER 14

THE POWER OF FAITH

One thing is for certain- without faith nothing can get accomplished. I need faith, you need faith, God desires that we live by faith in His Son Jesus Christ. When we repented of our sins and believed in Jesus Christ as our Lord and Savior, we received God's Holy Spirit into our lives. His Spirit became one with our spirit. We became brand new creations in Christ Jesus. His Holy Spirit is a divine engine within us that enables us to do what God called us to do and be who God called us to be. When we accepted Jesus Christ we received the ability to live and walk in supernatural faith. It's part of our new identity in Christ Jesus to live and walk in the same faith that Jesus Christ walked in through our new identity in Christ Jesus.

The Bible says, "faith comes by hearing and hearing by the word of God." It also says that "faith without action is dead." One of the ways our faith grows is by hearing the word of God and getting a revelation of the word of God. As we get revelation of the Word of God, our faith grows. Another way your faith grows is by mixing action with your faith. Mixing action with your faith includes obeying the word of God, stepping out in faith, and doing what He tells you to do. God desires that we use our faith, that we do what He says, and that we step out to live out His calling for our lives out of a personal relationship with Him. All of this is accomplished by faith in Him, trusting in Him, putting all of our reliance on Him, and yielding to His voice.

It is key for you to understand that God not only loves you but God also believes in you. Jesus Christ is tangible evidence of that divine truth. That is so awesome that God has faith in you, He believes in you. When He sent His Son Jesus Christ to die for you, shed

His blood for you, and rise from the dead on the third day victorious for you, He had faith that you would have faith in His Son Jesus. It is amazing that God has faith in His creation. That ought to ignite your faith and cause faith to rise up in you. I want you to confess this with me with a smile, "God loves me, He believes in me, He celebrates me, He is for me, and not against me."

God desires that we pray from a position of faith, with complete trust and confidence in Him, and all of our reliance on Him, with joyful expectation. He desires that we read our Bibles from a position of faith and declare the word of God from a position of faith. He wants us to praise and worship Him, and share Him with the world from a position of faith. He desires that we live with an inward knowing that He is faithful, that He is on our side, that He is for us, that He is our Heavenly Father, and that we are His children in Christ Jesus. God desires that we wake up in faith, go throughout our day in faith, and that we even sleep in faith. He desires that we use our God-given gift of free will to *choose* to live a life of faith in Him. He desires that we reject fear, all lies from the defeated devil, and we choose to live a life of faith Monday through Sunday. We, the body of Christ, are a people of faith, hope, and love.

Do not tolerate doubt, anxiety, or unbelief. Reject it and do not accept it. Like I said in some of the other chapters, if you begin to think on or detect negative thoughts, use your mouth and declare the word of God over your life to where it forces your brain and emotions to explode with joy, peace, hope, and faith. Take your faith and joy seriously. Take your thought life seriously. Faith is a key component to do what God called you to do. You are a person of faith! Your trust is not in this world, your trust is in JESUS! Your trust is in GOD! Your trust is in His promises! Your trust is in His Word and faithfulness to it!

It is vital that you remember that faith is not waiting for a feeling to step out. Remember we are not led by our feelings. We are led by the Holy Spirit of God and we move in *faith*. A simple example of this is not waiting to feel like praying to pray or waiting to read the Bible until you feel like doing so. Do not wait to feel like praising and worshiping God to praise and worship Him! Do not wait to feel like stepping out into what God has called you to do so! Step out and *do* it. Accomplish the tasks He has planned for you to do whether you feel like it or not.

Often once you take that first step of faith, the feelings of faith, joy, and confidence that you desire will soon follow. The point is this- do not wait for the feelings to step out in faith. No matter how you feel, choose to be led by the Holy Spirit of God, sensitive to His inward promptings. Tap into the joy of the Lord Jesus by faith. Tap into the joy of being saved by grace through faith in Jesus, the joy of being forgiven through repentance of sins and faith in Jesus Christ, and the joy of everlasting life through faith in Jesus. Receive the joy of being a citizen of Heaven, a child of God, and ambassador of the Kingdom of God in Christ Jesus. Tap into the joy of the Lord Jesus Christ by *faith*. Rejoice and praise God before your prayers are even answered. When you pray, believe that God is hearing you. Worship God from a celebratory, joyful place with whole-hearted trust in God, knowing that He is faithful.

David had faith in God when he killed Goliath the giant. Moses had faith in God when He was used as a tool to save and lead five million Israelites through the waters that God split. Jesus Christ had faith, the disciples had faith, every single person who was used by God in the Bible had faith in Him. They each obeyed His voice and mixed their faith with action. We too are called to live a life of faith. I encourage you to choose faith, listen to the word of God, and get revelation by the Holy Spirit's enlightenment of His Word so your faith can grow. Combine your faith with action, knowing that God is faithful. Live out of your personal relationship with Him. Get to know Him through prayer, His Word, and worship unto Him.

Everything that the Lord has accomplished through my life over the years was accomplished by grace through faith in Jesus Christ. By *faith* I was able to graduate from Rhema Bible Training Center and Oral Roberts University. By *faith* I I started my God-given organization, Saving Our Generation Ministries. By *faith* I have been able to host evangelistic events, release albums, music videos, and different kingdom projects. By *faith* I have reached millions of people with the glorious Gospel of Jesus Christ. It all happened by grace through faith in Jesus Christ, for the glory of God. It was a direct result of putting my trust and faith in God. It happened by mixing faith with action. All the various things that God is calling me to do in the future will also happen by grace through faith in Him.

Choose to live a life of radiating, explosive, joyful, celebratory faith in God! Choose to put all of your trust in Jesus Christ. Stay excited about the things of God, knowing that you are a person of faith. Below, there is a faith confession the Lord had me put together. I want you to confess it over your life. There are also some Bible verses that will help build your faith and I encourage you to read them. Let them encourage and minister to you. The next chapter is a chapter called "Step Out." It is going to encourage you in the call of God on your life. It is going to help you to step out and be used by God. It will help equip you to bring Heaven to earth through preaching, teaching, living, and demonstrating the Glorious Gospel of Jesus Christ. It will encourage you to be the hands and feet of Jesus. Get ready because it is going to be a major blessing to you! I love you, I believe in you, and I am cheering you on!

KINGDOM FAITH CONFESSION:
Declare This With Me:
"I am a person of faith. My faith is in Jesus. God is on my side. God is with me. God has my back. Everything is working out in my favor because I am a Child of God in Christ Jesus. God is my Heavenly Father. All of my trust is in God. My faith is in the word of God. My faith is in the promises of God. I

am blessed because Jesus Christ lives on the inside of me. Resurrection power is on the inside of me in Christ Jesus. I am moving forward in the grace of God. I live a life of repentance and faith in Jesus. I live a life of the Bible. I live a life of prayer. I live a life of praise and worship unto God. I live a life of forgiveness. I live a life of eternal hope in Christ Jesus. God's love has been shed abroad in my heart. I live from God's love. God's love is my fuel. God's love is my "why" and God's love is my motive. God's love for me proven through the life, bloodshed, death, and resurrection of Jesus Christ is my gasoline. I am God's wonderful beautiful creation and I am made in His image. I am prosperous in Christ Jesus. I am strong in Christ Jesus. I am healthy. I am blessed. I have no lack in Christ Jesus. I am forgiven in Christ Jesus. I am righteous in Christ Jesus. I am God's royalty in Christ Jesus. I have royal blood flowing through my veins in Christ Jesus. I am a citizen of Heaven in Christ Jesus. I am part of the body of Christ and I am part of the family of God. My identity is in Christ Jesus and I live from that reality. I have authority in Christ and I use the authority He has given me. I live one day at a time with an attitude of gratitude. I am living out God's plan for my life. I preach, teach, live, and demonstrate the Glorious Gospel of Jesus Christ. Everywhere I go, Jesus goes with me. Everywhere I go, His love, and presence go with me. I live in the fruits of the Holy Spirit. I live in the gifts of the Holy Spirit. I live in the joy of the Lord Jesus. I live in the kindness of the Lord Jesus. I live in the peace of the Lord Jesus. I live one step at a time,

one moment at a time, full of faith in the Lord Jesus Christ. In Christ Jesus my past, present, and future is bright. I praise God for the past, present, and future. I am led by God's Holy Spirit in all things. I go from glory to glory and faith to faith in Christ Jesus. I am an ambassador of the Kingdom of God. I am a person of Faith."

I want to encourage you to do faith-based Bible confessions daily! Feel free to confess this faith-based Bible confession every morning and make it part of your daily devotions! Confess God's word over your life in faith throughout the day! In Christ Jesus we go from faith to faith and glory to glory! Hallelujah to the most high God!

Let These Bible Verses Encourage You

"Now faith is the substance of things hoped for, the evidence of things not seen."
Hebrews 11:1

"That he would grant you, according to the riches of his glory, to be strengthened with might by his Spirit in the inner man; That Christ may dwell in your hearts by faith; that ye, being rooted and grounded in love"
Ephesians 3:16-17

"For we walk by faith, not by sight."
2 Corinthians 5:7

"But without faith it is impossible to please him: for he that cometh to God must believe that he is, and that he is a rewarder of them that diligently seek him."
Hebrews 11:6

"For by grace are ye saved through faith; and that not of yourselves: it is the gift of God: Not of works, lest any man should boast."
Ephesians 2:8-9

"Trust in the Lord with all thine heart; and lean not unto thine own understanding. In all thy ways acknowledge him, and he shall direct thy paths." Proverbs 3:5-6

"Knowing this, that the trying of your faith worketh patience."
James 1:3

"Whom having not seen, ye love; in whom, though now ye see him not, yet believing, ye rejoice with joy unspeakable and full of glory: Receiving the end of your faith, even the salvation of your souls." 1 Peter 1:8-9

"'If you can'?" said Jesus. "Everything is possible for one who believes."
Mark 9:23

"So then faith cometh by hearing, and hearing by the word of God."
Romans 10:17

"Jesus said unto her, I am the resurrection, and the life: he that believeth in me, though he were dead, yet shall he live: And whosoever liveth and believeth in me shall never die. Believest thou this?"
John 11:25-26

"And all things, whatsoever ye shall ask in prayer, believing, ye shall receive." Matthew 21:22

"And Jesus said unto him, Go thy way; thy faith hath made thee whole. And immediately he received his sight, and followed Jesus in the way." Mark 10:52

"And Jesus said unto them, I am the bread of life: he that cometh to me shall never hunger; and he that believeth on me shall never thirst." John 6:35

"Through faith also Sara herself received strength to conceive seed, and was delivered of a child when she was past age, because she judged him faithful who had promised." Hebrews 11:11

"For therein is the righteousness of God revealed from faith to faith: as it is written, The just shall live by faith." Romans 1:17

"For ye are all the children of God by faith in Christ Jesus. For as many of you as have been baptized into Christ have put on Christ." Galatians 3:26-27

"For God so loved the world, that he gave his only begotten Son, that whosoever believeth in him should not perish, but have everlasting life." John 3:16

"Is any sick among you? let him call for the elders of the church; and let them pray over him, anointing him with oil in the name of the Lord: And the prayer of faith shall save the sick, and the Lord shall raise him up; and if he have committed sins, they shall be forgiven him." James 5:14-15

"And Jesus said unto them, Because of your unbelief: for verily I say unto you, If ye have faith as a grain of mustard seed, ye shall say unto this mountain, Remove hence to yonder place; and it shall remove; and nothing shall be impossible unto you."
Matthew 17:20

"For verily I say unto you, That whosoever shall say unto this mountain, Be thou removed, and be thou cast into the sea; and shall not doubt in his heart, but shall believe that those things which he saith shall come to pass; he shall have whatsoever he saith." Mark11:23

"Jesus answered and said unto them, This is the work of God, that ye believe on him whom he hath sent." John 6:29

"He that believeth on me, as the scripture hath said, out of his belly shall flow rivers of living water." John 7:38

"For the scripture saith, Whosoever believeth on him shall not be ashamed." Romans 10:11

"Jesus saith unto him, Thomas, because thou hast seen me, thou hast believed: blessed are they that have not seen, and yet have believed." John 20:29

"But when Jesus heard it, he answered him, saying, Fear not: believe only, and she shall be made whole." Luke 8:50

"Therefore being justified by faith, we have peace with God through our Lord Jesus Christ." Romans 5:1

"Therefore I say unto you, What things soever ye desire, when ye pray, believe that ye receive them, and ye shall have them."
Mark 11:24

"But let him ask in faith, nothing wavering. For he that wavereth is like a wave of the sea driven with the wind and tossed." James 1:6

CHAPTER 15
STEP OUT

In your city there are lost, dying, hurting, depressed, tormented, confused people on the way to hell. I have been to the nation of Brazil twenty-five times, visited thirty cities, on evangelistic trips and ministered all over the United States of America. Anyone who knows me knows that I have been sharing the Gospel of Jesus Christ since the moment I surrendered my life to Christ in 2007. I started off sharing Jesus in my city, then my state, then my nation the USA. God then sent me to the nations of the world. If you profess to be a Christian and a disciple of Jesus Christ, the great commission in Matthew 28 is for you. Preaching, teaching, living, and demonstrating the glorious Gospel of Jesus Christ is for you. It starts with your home, your neighborhood, your block. It starts where you work, it starts where you are. You are a carrier of the glorious Gospel of Jesus Christ. Where you go, He goes with you. Where you go, His presence goes with you.

In 1 Corinthians 3 we see that, "some plant, some water, but God gives the increase." In order for that to happen, you and I must step out in faith. Tell people about how Jesus Christ translated you from the kingdom of darkness into His beloved kingdom of Light. Share your Jesus testimony and how God could do the same for them. Release a word of encouragement from God's Holy Word over people you meet. Share the divine message of Jesus Christ. Pray with people to repent of their sins and put their faith in Him for Salvation. Pray with people to put their faith in Jesus so that they can receive everything He made available with His blood. The reality is it, it takes you stepping out in faith and opening up your mouth, no matter how you feel.

I have heard the statement, "Preach the Gospel of Jesus Christ, and if necessary use words." I understand that and agree with that in context. The reality is though, it takes you proclaiming and explaining the Gospel out of your mouth, and praying with people so that they can receive salvation in Christ. Of course, live the Gospel with your heart, live the Gospel with your thoughts, and live the Gospel with your actions. However, in the midst of that, do not forget that opening your mouth to share the Gospel is also a major part that needs to joyfully be done.

Oftentimes I think about what Jesus Christ accomplished through His life, His bloodshed, His death, and resurrection. I ponder on how he defeated death, hell, and the grave, how he defeated satan and his demons. I think about what I received by the repentance and confessing of my sins, what I received by putting my faith in Jesus Christ. I think about how He saved me, gave me everlasting life, healed me, forgave me, washed me clean, set me free, made me a new creation in Him, engrafted me into His glorious Kingdom, adopted me into His family, put His royal eternal blood in my veins, made Heaven my eternal destination, putting Heaven on the inside of me. I meditate on how He became my Heavenly Father, made me His Son, gave me access to a personal relationship with Him, put His Holy Spirit in me, and enabled me to walk in His gifts and fruits. Read 1 Corinthians 12 and Galatians 5:22-23 to learn about those gifts and fruits of the Holy Spirit. When I think about how He placed His abilities, His Spirit, and His empowerment on the inside of me, THERE IS NO WAY I can keep my mouth shut and not share the GLORIOUS GREAT NEWS of JESUS CHRIST with this dying and hurting world. There is no way that I can keep my mouth shut and not share with people that through repentance of sins and faith in Jesus Christ as Lord and Savior, they too can receive the glorious redemption package of Heaven.

Some may say, "I want to but I am afraid," or "I want to but I do not know how." Some may say "I have the desire to but right when I am about to, I take a step back." Well, I have good news for every disciple of Jesus who is reading this that has not been sharing the Gospel of Jesus Christ or simply needs some encouragement in this area. In the next paragraphs, I am going to give you a basic outline and set of steps on how to share your faith. Before I do that, I want to remind you once again about some biblical truth that you might have heard me share before. I dare you to keep reading the rest of this book and I pray the Holy Spirit fire and power consumes every part of your life and that the boldness of God consumes you right now, in Jesus' Name.

God desires that you live in communion with Him. I like to call it, "unbroken fellowship with God's Holy Spirit." God desires that you live out of your personal relationship with Him. There is nothing more exciting, fun, and adventurous than a real life-breathing, life-giving, personal relationship with Him. This does not mean that external situations and circumstances are always going to be easy. This just means that GOD, the maker of the universe, is on the inside of you, in Christ Jesus. What that means is that you can handle and overcome anything with ease when you do it through *His* strength. His yoke is easy and His burden is light.

There is nothing greater than a personal relationship with the true living God through repentance of sins, by grace through faith in His son Jesus Christ, through His Holy Spirit who dwells in you. Out of your relationship with Him, your identity in Him, and your authority in Him, is where you live, move, and have your being. If you profess to be a Christian and a disciple of Jesus Christ, you should be embracing, enjoying, and reading the Bible every day. You should be joyfully praying and talking to God every day. You should be worshiping Him, praising Him, and singing songs to Him every day. You should be renewing your mind with His word, speaking His promises out of your mouth in confidence, every day. You should be doing this throughout the day, staying in communion with Him. Out of this place is where you preach, teach, live, and demonstrate the glorious Gospel of Jesus Christ.

Never start your day without communing with God through prayer, worship and the Bible. Start the day with the Holy Spirit and take authority over your day in Christ Jesus. Do it by decreeing and declaring victory over your day, praying what the Holy Spirit desires to pray through you. Declare life over your day and what He desires to happen that day in Christ Jesus. Out of your mouth proclaim protection, pleading the blood of Jesus, canceling all accidents, mistakes, and human error, at the name of Jesus. Take authority over your day every morning.

I have been sold out to Jesus Christ and all-in with the kingdom of God for over fourteen years now and I can say that there is nothing more fulfilling than living out of your relationship with God. There is nothing more worthwhile than investing in eternity, investing into the kingdom of God by preaching, teaching, living, and demonstrating the glorious Gospel of Jesus Christ. There is nothing more satisfying than living a life of faith and confidence in the true living God. It is so fulfilling to pick someone up who fell and save them, through Christ. True joy comes when you minister healing to those who are hurting, give food to the hungry, and clothe those who are naked. There is no greater feeling than allowing Jesus Christ to meet someone else's need through using your life.

Every day you walk past people who are hurting confused, and tormented in their minds, dealing with suicidal spirits. Every day you will come across someone who is tormented by demons, someone who is lost, depressed, and on the way to hell. God desires you to pour into them through his Holy Spirit. God desires that you pour into people you encounter every single day. He wants to use you to bring the light of Christ, the light of Heaven, and the light of the Kingdom of God to this hurting world.

Twenty Simple Ways To Be Used By God

1. Develop a sensitivity to God's voice. You do this by building a personal relationship with Him, through praise and worship, the Bible, prayer. This is done through renewing your mind with His word, through speaking it in faith, from the first person.

2. Live out of your personal relationship with God. Remember the Bible says in Acts 17:28, "In Him you move, live, and have your being."

3. Realize that the results are up to *God*. Your part is simply stepping out and being sensitive to what God desires to say and do through you, as you minister to a lost soul, prodigal son or daughter.

4. Step out no matter how you feel. simply open up your mouth and share in faith, trusting and believing that God is going to use you. Emotions usually change due to outward circumstances and situations. Do not allow your emotions to direct your life. Let the Spirit of God direct your life and live in faith, knowing the feelings will eventually catch up to what you believe. What you believe is the everlasting living Word of God.

By utilizing the weaponry that God has given you in Christ Jesus, you can live in the emotions of Heaven. These emotions of heaven include peace, joy, and excitement cannot be expressed in words. Be led by the internal peace of the Holy Spirit. Follow His inward internal promptings. He is a divine navigation system that God has made available to you. Simply step out and let God use you no matter how you feel. Be led by the Holy Spirit of God. He has anointed you for such a time as this, in Christ.

5. Remember what Jesus said when He was recruiting His disciples. He said He was going to make them into "fishers of men." Evangelizing and sharing Jesus is similar to fishing, except instead of fishing for fish, you are fishing for souls with pure and biblical motives. Be sensitive as you are ministering to people. Whether you are listening to what they have to say or speaking into their lives, be led by the Holy Spirit in all that you do. At the right moment pull the hook. Look in their eyes and ask them if they want to repent of their sins and put their faith in Jesus. As they say yes, stretch out your hand with God and grab theirs and pray with them a prayer of repentance and faith in Jesus. Step twenty on this list is an example of a prayer you can pray with them. Whether it is a first time salvation or a prodigal son or daughter coming back to God's Kingdom, rededicating their lives to Jesus, step out and allow God to use you. Another simple strategy is to ask them if they need any prayer in a specific area of their life. If they say yes, pray about it in faith and believe for the miracle. Attach your faith with their faith in Jesus. Let God do what He does! Hallelujah!

6. Remember that planting and watering seeds of God's Kingdom can be done in several ways. You can offer a listening ear, share your testimony about how Jesus Christ transformed your life, and how He can do the same thing for them. You can speak a Biblical word of encouragement over their lives. You can preach the story of Jesus and share what He made available through faith in Him. Pray with them to repent of their sins and put their faith in Jesus Christ, so that they can begin their personal relationship with God. You can ask them how their relationship with God currently is and their answer alone will open a door for you to speak into their lives and point them to JESUS. Take the pressure off of yourself by recognizing the results are up to *God*. Remember in the Bible one thief that was next to Jesus Christ on the cross accepted Him, repented of sins, and believed in Him. And the other rejected Him. Some will accept what you have to say to them and some will reject it. Leave the results up to God. Simply do your part and step out. Inviting them to your Church or an evangelistic event is always an easy way to break the ice before ministering to them. Always give them an opportunity to repent of their sins and surrender their hearts to Jesus. Offer them the opportunity to dedicate their lives to Him, receive Jesus Christ as Lord and Savior of their lives. The Bible says in 2 Corinthians 6:2 that, "Today is the day of salvation." By faith, we can have a vision for tomorrow, but God ultimately knows what tomorrow holds.

7. As you step out, remember God's glory is in you, on you, and ready to flow through you. Remember that everything you do, you do it unto the Lord. Instead of doing it out of selfish ambition, everything you do must be done for the glory and honor of the Lord. You do it to praise and worship the true living God of Abraham.

8. As you step out, remember it is about being kingdom of God-minded and body of Christ-minded. That means that when someone receives salvation by repenting of sins and putting their faith in Jesus Christ, that is a WIN for the kingdom of God, and not just a WIN for you. That is a WIN for the body of Christ. Any advancement and growth of God's Kingdom is a WIN for the entire Kingdom of God and the entire body of Christ. At the end of the day, the glory does not go to a specific man or woman that is being used by God, but to God alone! He alone is worthy of the praise, honor, and glory. Everything you do from the moment you wake up, throughout the day, and even when you sleep, you do it unto the Lord. As you step out to win souls for Jesus, to plant eternal seeds of God's Kingdom into people's hearts, remember all the glory, praise, and honor goes to Him. Hallelujah! We celebrate as the body of Christ and we celebrate as God's Kingdom. We praise Him together anytime there is any advancement, and growth of His Kingdom. It is all about being Kingdom of God-minded and body of Christ-minded.

9. As you pray with people to repent of their sins and put their faith in Jesus Christ, pray with them to dedicate and surrender their hearts and lives to Christ. Right when you say "in Jesus' Name, Amen," look into their eyes and smile at them. Congratulate them and welcome them into the kingdom of God. Welcome them into the body of Christ. Do it in the joy of the Lord Jesus Christ! Ask them if they have a home church and if they do not have one, invite them to go to your church that upcoming Sunday. Show them how to download the "YouVersion" bible app on their phones. If they do not have a phone, find a way to get them a physical Bible. Encourage everyone to have a hardback

Bible and to have daily devotions and live for God. See how you can get them plugged into your church and discipled. Share with them on how your relationship with God has impacted your life. Every disciple of Jesus should have a home church where they can worship God and grow spiritually with other believers. No matter what Church you go to it is KEY to understand that as a Christian and disciple of Jesus Christ, we are all part of the same eternal family of God. We are all part of God's Kingdom in Christ Jesus. We are all part of the Body of Christ no matter what Christ-centered and Bible-centered church that you are a member of. We are each a part of the same team, army, and eternal force that cannot be stopped in Christ Jesus. We are the victorious, glorious, radiant, eternal Kingdom of God.

10. Remember to keep the main thing the main thing.. LOVE GOD, LOVE PEOPLE, HATE EVIL. Jesus Christ said, "Love God with all of your heart, all your mind, all your soul, and all your will and love your neighbor as you love yourself." He said, "On these two commandments hang all the laws of the prophets." I encourage you to read Matthew 22:35-40, Mark 12:28-31, and Luke 10:27 to read more about this. God desires that you meditate on the life, bloodshed, death, and resurrection of Jesus Christ. As you do that, you are able to continually catch greater insight on how much He loves you, desires a relationship with you, and how your identity is in *Him*. From that place, you will be empowered to love God with all your heart, all your mind, all your soul, and will. You will then be able to love your neighbor in ways you never could on your own. From that place, you are empowered to live a life of forgiveness and be a peacemaker. Remember God's love in you is what enables you to see people through

His love. His love empowers you to believe and assume the best about all people at all times. Remember you cannot do this in your own ability, strength, or power. It is out of His ability, His strength, His identity and empowerment in you, that you are able to live out the Christian life. You cannot live the Christian life without Christ Himself living through you. You cannot live the Christian life unless you live it out of your relationship with Him. Allow the life, bloodshed, death, and resurrection of Jesus Christ to radically draw you and empower you to seek God like you never sought Him before. Allow it to radically inspire and motivate you to step out in what He has called you to be. Allow it to radically encourage you to pray, worship Him, read your Bible, renew your mind with His word, and declare it out of your mouth. Allow it to stir something up on the inside of you to share the Gospel with someone every single day. It will help you bring the light of Christ to this hurting world.

11. Remember the Bible says in 1 John 4:4 that, "Greater is He who lives in you than he that is in the world." Jesus Christ defeated the devil with a score of one hundred to zero. He stripped satan of all his power. The only power the devil has is the power you give him through sin, breaking God's laws. Sin includes lying, stealing, cheating, gossip, envy, unforgiveness, fornication, immorality, and drug or alcohol addiction. Through unrepentant sin and meditating on the devil's lies instead of the TRUTH of God's Word, the defeated devil has access to torment people. Sin gives legal access for demons to invade and torment one's life. The defeated devil's mission is to kill, steal, and destroy you. Christ's mission is to give you life and give it to you more abundantly in Him, according to John 10:10. Christ's mission is to restore you, save you, heal you, and the beautiful eternal list goes on. Repenting and confessing your sins, putting faith in Jesus Christ as Lord and Savior, living in unbroken fellowship and communion with the Holy Spirit, is how you live untouched by the devil and his demons. Remember in Ephesians 2:6 the Bible says that you are "seated in Heavenly places with Christ Jesus, far above every demonic force." When you worship God in Spirit and in truth, demons flee. When you read the Bible out loud, demons flee. When you pray in your native language (English, Spanish, etc), or in the language of the Holy Spirit, tongues, demons flee. When you repent of your sins, put faith in Jesus, call demonic spirits by name and rebuke them at the name of Jesus, demons flee. Remember that you are God's representative on the earth, equipped, empowered, and chosen for such a time as this. You were born to make an eternal difference on this planet for the kingdom of God through proclamation, explanation, living, and demonstrating the glorious Gospel of Jesus Christ.

12. Abide in the love of God, live in the love of God, spread the love of God. Abide and live in the mercy of God; spread the mercy of God. Abide in the Truth of God's Word, spread the truth of His word, and live in that truth. Abide in the faith of God, live in the faith of God, and spread it across the world. Abide in the unity of God, live in the unity of God, and share that unity with others. Abide in and live out the gospel of Jesus Christ. The Christian life was created to be lived out by faith in   JESUS. You were saved by grace, through faith, in Jesus Christ. When you pray, pray in faith. When you worship God, worship Him in faith. When you read the Bible, read the Bible in faith. When you confess God's word through your mouth, confess it in faith. When you share the glorious Gospel of Jesus

Christ, share it believing that it is going to penetrate through the hearts of who you are sharing it with. The Bible says that the righteous shall live by faith. Believe the best, expect the best, assume the best, and do your part as God's best manifests. Live a life of faith and put your trust in God. Hallelujah!

13. Allow God's love that was demonstrated through the life, bloodshed, death, and resurrection of Jesus Christ to empower you to forgive every person who has ever done you wrong in the past, present, or future. Live in the forgiveness of God. Release grudges; do not hold onto them. A life of forgiveness is a life of freedom. Abide in the forgiveness of God, live in the forgiveness of God, and show the forgiveness of God to all people. Do it by faith. God loves you so much and Jesus Christ is tangible evidence of this undeniable truth. Confess this with me by faith. Say, "I forgive every single person who hurt me in the past in the mighty Name of Jesus. God, I ask you to show mercy and love to them. God, I ask you to show love and mercy to me." Declare this with me, "I am a person of forgiveness, faith, hope, and love." Hallelujah!

14. Live a righteous, pure, holy, and sanctified life in Christ Jesus. Do it out of your personal relationship with Him. Remember you are an ambassador of God's Kingdom. Be alert with what you say, how you live, and how you carry yourself. You are an ambassador of the kingdom of God. Avoid evil; avoid even the appearance of evil. Remember you are a carrier of God's glory and your God-given body is the temple of the Holy Spirit. The last thing you would ever want to do is hinder someone from surrendering to Jesus Christ. You would never want to grieve the Holy Spirit. Live a life that glorifies God, from your motives, the thoughts that you think, words that you speak, and your actions. I pray God's love & light will continue to shine in and through your life, in the mighty name of Jesus.

15. You were called to a life of progression in Christ Jesus. You were called to a life of repentance and faith in Christ Jesus. You were called to continually grow in your relationship with Jesus. If you fall or mess up, get back up, repent of your sins, and put your faith in Jesus Christ. Remember you have a mediator and His Name is Jesus Christ of Nazareth. He is our divine Savior, Redeemer, and King of Kings, the Son of God. He gives you the access and ability to be reconciled back to God, restored back to relationship with Him, and resurrected in Christ Jesus. Through faith in Him, you are one with Him, and He is one with you. God desires that you have a heart for Him. This means that who He is and what He is about is your number one desire. This means that what He desires is what *your* heart desires. Live with a heart for God, a passion for Him and everything He is about. Cultivate a deep passion for God and spread it throughout the world.

16. Remember to take one day at a time, and one moment at a time. Live in the moment, live in the now. There is nothing wrong with having vision for the future, but you can only live in the now. Make the voice of the Holy Spirit your number one priority. Continually grow in your sensitivity to His voice by building a relationship with Him through prayer, worship, and the Bible. Continually do everything you can to be faithful to Him. Yield to Him, and his voice. Allow Him to guide and direct you in all things. Remember to enjoy your relationship with God, enjoy the journey, have fun with it. Step out and be the answer to someone's prayer.

Step out and manifest the glorious Gospel of Jesus Christ.

17. Remember that there are lost souls and hurting people everywhere. Those lost souls are looking for fulfillment, validation, verification, identity, and love in all the wrong places. They do not know that true fulfillment, validation, identity, and love could only be found in a personal relationship with God. They do not know that it is found in a life of praise and worship unto the true living God. They are not aware that it is found in a life of embracing and reading the Bible, prayer and talking to God. They do not know that there is power in speaking the word of God and that there is divine healing made available through His Word, the presence of God, and through the name of Jesus. Many are unaware that there is supernatural healing made available through identifying with Jesus Christ and being a new creation in Him. The reality is we *do* know and it is our job to be the bridge and point them to Jesus Christ by sharing His kingdom with them. We must share the Gospel with them so they can be saved, healed, set free, and delivered for the glory of God! Hallelujah! It is our responsibility to share the good news of Jesus Christ with them so they can begin to live a victorious, overcoming life in Him. Once we share that, they can then be used by God and make an eternal difference through their lives in Christ Jesus. When your relationship with God is thriving, vibrant, and alive, it will leak over into all your other relationships and friendships. You will notice that victory will invade every area of your life. When you seek God's kingdom first and His righteousness, you will see that everything else will be added, according to His will.

18. Preach the Gospel. Teach the Gospel. Live and demonstrate the Gospel. Heal the sick, drive out demons, and raise the dead. Plant seeds, water seeds, and allow God to bring the increase. Step out, trust in Him, and let Him use you. Remember God is with you, He loves you and He is for you. You are not alone. You are a part of God's kingdom, an eternal force that cannot be stopped! Hallelujah! Step out and allow God to use you! There are souls attached to your "yes" to Jesus. All the people that God has allowed me to reach were attached to my "yes" to Jesus. All the people that God has called me to reach in the future are attached to my "yes" to Jesus, and all the people that God called you to reach are connected to your "yes" to Jesus. They are a result of you yielding to and being faithful to His voice. The fulfillment of God's plans and purposes for our lives is directly connected to our "yes" to Him. Faith mixed with corresponding action to His voice and Word is truly alive.

19. Choose to be grateful instead of complaining. Remember to be a peacemaker instead of bringing strife and gossip. Speak life instead of speaking death. Bring love instead of bringing hate. Remember that the only reason you can be used by God is through grace in Christ Jesus. Get excited! Get excited! Get excited! What a day to be alive, step out, let God use you, and be the solution to the world's problems, in Christ Jesus. Share the glorious gospel of Jesus Christ. Remember that every industry or job is a mission field, every city is a mission field. The earth is a mission field, wherever you go is your mission field!

20. Salvation and Rededication Prayer For You Personally Or For You To Pray With Someone:

Confess this with me, "God I ask you for forgiveness of every sin I have ever committed. Forgive me for opening doors to demonic activity through sin. I put my faith in your Son, Jesus Christ. I confess with my mouth and believe with my heart that He is my Lord and Savior. I believe that He is your Son, I believe that He is The Messiah, I believe that He rose from the dead victorious on the third day. Jesus Christ, I receive your grace, I receive everything you made available through your life, bloodshed, death, resurrection, and ascension into Heaven, at the right hand of God. Holy Spirit, I ask that you baptize me, fill me with your love, fire, and with your power. Holy Spirit, I ask you to fill me to the overflow. God, I ask you to make my life a demonstration of your grace, love, and power. I cancel and break every demonic chain and stronghold in the name of Jesus Christ attached through decisions I have made in the past. I command every demonic force and demonic entity to leave in the name of Jesus Christ. I dedicate my heart, my mind, my emotions, my body, my life, my house, everything I own to you, Jesus Christ. Holy Spirit, I give you complete access to every aspect of my life. From this day on, I will live for you with all of my heart, all of my thoughts, all of my emotions, all of my body, and all of my life unto you, the true living God. My past, my present, and my future is bright because I have become one with you, Jesus Christ. Hallelujah in the mighty name of Jesus Christ, Amen".

Let These Bible Verses Encourage You

"This is the covenant that I will make with them after those days, saith the Lord, I will put my laws into their hearts, and in their minds will I write them."
Hebrews 10:16

"And hope maketh not ashamed; because the love of God is shed abroad in our hearts by the Holy Ghost which is given unto us." Romans 5:5

"Therefore if any man be in Christ, he is a new creature: old things are passed away; behold, all things are become new." 2 Corinthians 5:17

"And now abideth faith, hope, charity, these three; but the greatest of these is love." 1 Corinthians 13:13

"We love him, because he first loved us." 1 John 4:19

"For the wages of sin is death; but the gift of God is eternal life through Jesus Christ our Lord." Romans 6:23

"And these signs shall follow them that believe; In my name shall they cast out devils; they shall speak with new tongues." Mark16:17

"For God so loved the world, that he gave his only begotten Son, that whosoever believeth in him should not perish, but have everlasting life. For God sent not his Son into the world to condemn the world; but that the world through him might be saved." John 3:16-17

"For as many as are led by the Spirit of God, they are the sons of God." Romans 8:14

"Ye are of God, little children, and have overcome them: because greater is he that is in you, than he that is in the world." 1 John 4:4

"And he said unto them, Go ye into all the world, and preach the gospel to every creature." Mark 16:15

"And they went forth, and preached every where, the Lord working with them, and confirming the word with signs following. Amen." Mark 16:20

"For therein is the righteousness of God revealed from faith to faith: as it is written, The just shall live by faith." Romans 1:17

"For whosoever shall call upon the name of the Lord shall be saved." Romans 10:13

"Say not ye, There are yet four months, and then cometh harvest? behold, I say unto you, Lift up your eyes, and look on the fields; for they are white already to harvest." John 4:35

CHAPTER 16

Unveiling GOD'S KINGDOM & EXPOSING the devil's kingdom

After you repented of your sins and put your faith in Jesus Christ as Lord and Savior, you became a brand new creation in Christ. Old things passed away and all things became new. In your new identity in Christ Jesus, you have realities such as eternal life, forgiveness of sins, salvation, etc. By putting your faith in Jesus Christ as Lord and Savior, you received many spiritual blessings, gifts, and new realities. Another one of those new creation in-Christ realities that you have access to is the casting out of demons at the name of Jesus Christ. There is salvation in Jesus, forgiveness in Jesus, eternal life in Jesus, and demons flee at the name of Jesus when you cast them out.

Praise and worship is your weapon. Reading the Bible, prayer, speaking God's Word, and gratitude are some weapons. But casting out demons and rebuking them at the name of Jesus is also a weapon that you possess! It is not dangerous to have an enemy. It is dangerous to not know *who* your enemy is, *how* He operates, how to *cast* him out and *keep* him out. Jesus Christ casted out demons, His disciples casted out demons, and the early church casted out demons. Without a doubt, every believer and follower of Christ needs to know how to cast out demons and live the victorious life in Christ Jesus.

When you cast out demons at the name of Jesus Christ, ask God to give you discernment on what kind of spirit it is. Demonic spirits include depression, fear, anxiety, doubt, sickness, perversion, fornication, death, immorality, suicide, jealousy, envy, unforgiveness, gossip, confusion, hatred, etc. When you rebuke and cast out the demon, do it in faith at the name of Jesus Christ. Do it from your identity in Him, conscious of who you are in Him, and that you are seated with Him in Heavenly places, at the right hand of God, far above any demonic force or demonic principality. An example would be saying, "In the name of Jesus Christ, spirit of _______________, I command you to leave right now!" You may even feel something leave the room. When you do it, do it with authority, out of your identity in Christ. If you are casting it out of a person when you pray for them, you may feel something shift in the atmosphere. You may feel something leave. The person's countenance may change. They may feel that something left their body. There is power in the name of Jesus Christ that makes demons flee. We are a people of faith and we live by faith in the son of God, Jesus Christ. When you cast demons out, cast them out in faith at the name of Jesus. There is power in the name of Jesus Christ that breaks demonic chains and strongholds! You have the legal right to use the name of Jesus Christ as a born-again, new creation, in Christ (see 2 Corinthians 5:17). The defeated devil has no power over someone who knows who they are in Christ and knows their authority. The defeated devil is like a swatted fruit fly. The only power the defeated devil has is the power someone gives to him by living a life of darkness in sin, believing his lies, taking his offers of deceptions, yielding to his deceptive suggestions, etc.

You make ask, "Who is the devil and his demons?" According to the word, lucifer (the devil), is a fallen angel that wanted to dethrone God and take His place. He deceived one-third of the angels in heaven. God kicked him out of heaven and he fell "like lightning," along with one-third of the angels. Lucifer then became satan and the one-third of the angels that he deceived became his demons. They lost all their glory and everything that God gave them. They strayed away from their original purpose of being created. The devil and his demons hate humanity, God, and everything that God created.

The devil and his demons want to kill, steal, and destroy, according to John 10:10. They want to destroy everything that has to do with God and anything that He created. There are demon sectors and forces assigned to different negative things or sins. Their agenda and mission is to kill, steal, and destroy. Their agenda is to take humanity to hell, a place of eternal torture, torment, pain, and eternal separation from the true living God. Heaven is a place of everlasting joy, peace, excitement, unity, and eternal communion and fellowship with the true living God. Words cannot express the joy and peace of Heaven. Words also cannot express the pain and sadness of hell.

The proof that the devil and his demons exist is very simple. When you look around the earth today you will see the murder, violence, hatred, jealousy, robbery, suicide, immorality, adultery, fornication, division, negativity, abortion, prostitution, evil, etc. It is very easy to see the devil and his demons are at work. That is why you must understand who you are in Christ, your authority in Christ, and what gives demons legal access to someone's life. Demons can possess or have access to live inside a human body. They may control that person's mind and actions or oppress their mind, body and life.

What gives the devil and his demons legal access to someone's life? Breaking God's laws, doing things the devil's way instead of God's ways, is how this happens. Once again, a simple example of sin is lying, cheating, stealing, violence, unforgiveness, jealousy, fornication, pornography, immorality, perversion, gossip, pride, envy, etc. Your body is a house, your body is the temple of the Holy Spirit. When someone sins, they open the door to demonic spirits coming inside and tormenting them. Sin opens doors for demons to invade one's life. It gives them legal access to speak into your ears and influence your thoughts. By influencing your thoughts, they torment your mind and direct your decisions. Through this they even receive access to live inside one's body. Their agenda and assignment is to kill, steal, and destroy you.

Defeated demons only have the legal right to destroy your life if you open the door through sin with no repentance. They only have legal access to your life by you not repenting of and confessing your sins to God, asking Him for forgiveness, and putting your faith in Jesus Christ as Lord and Savior of your life. Repentance of sins and faith in Jesus is how you close the door to the defeated devil. Casting out and rebuking them at the name of Jesus causes demons to leave and flee your life. Unrepentant sin is how the door stays open and the demons have legal access to your life. That is why many people are tormented, depressed, suicidal, confused, defeated in their minds, etc. That is why one of the number one things that the devil hates is when a Christian lives in fellowship and communes with the Holy Spirit on a continual basis. Satan hates Christians that have a vibrant life of worship, prayer, reading the Bible, speaking the word of God. He hates when Christians speak the Word in faith, share Bible truths, preach, teach, and demonstrate the glorious Gospel of Jesus Christ. The devil hates the Christian that is in tune with the Holy Spirit of God, who wakes up in the morning, goes through his day, and goes to sleep filled with His Holy Spirit.

The devil cannot stand the Christian who is continually building and growing in their personal relationship with Jesus. A Christian who walks in love, forgives and lives in the fruits of the Holy Spirit out of their personal relationship with God, is satan's worst enemy. The devil hates a Christian that abides in the love of God and brings the light of Christ everywhere he or she goes. He cannot stand a Christian who runs to God and repents quickly after sinning. A Christian who goes after God with all of their heart, thoughts, emotions, mind, and will, is a threat to the devil.

The devil hates the Christian who keeps doors closed to him by living from their relationship with God, living a righteous, pure, life in Christ. He is threatened by the Christian who lives a life of pure motives, pure thoughts, and pure body, a life in which the purity of God flows in and through. The defeated devil hates a life that is empowered out of a personal relationship with God. The devil hates a life that is consumed in God's glory. The devil is threatened when lost people who are living in sin repent of their sins and put their faith in Jesus Christ and begin to live for God in all areas of their life.

You were created to know God and to make Him known. You were created to build a relationship with God and be filled with His Holy presence and His Holy Spirit. You were created for personal fellowship with God. He desires to flow in your life and through your life. Out of your personal relationship with Him, He wants to use you to bring the light of Heaven to this dark world. By repenting of your sins, confessing them to God, putting your faith in Jesus Christ as Lord and your Savior, your sins are washed away. You become a brand new creation in Christ, you receive everlasting life, Heaven becomes your eternal destination, you become forgiven, and God places His Holy Spirit on the inside of you. You identify with Jesus Christ, He gives you authority through Him to live a victorious life. When you speak it is as if He is speaking through you. When you say the name of Jesus Christ, demons flee. When you worship God, demons flee. When you speak the word of God, demons flee. When you read the Bible out loud, demons flee.

God desires that you live conscious of who you are in Him. He desires that you live a life of unbroken fellowship with Him, enabling you to live a life that is untouched by the devil and his demons. God desires that you live a victorious, overcoming life filled with His glory. God desires that you live with a renewed mind that is filled with His word. He wants your mind to be filled with what He said about you instead of what the world and the defeated devil says about you. God desires that you speak His word and declare His promises. By doing that, your mind is renewed and transformed continually into the way He thinks, where you will have "the mind of Christ."

God desires that you live out of identity in Him, seated in Heavenly places in Christ Jesus, far above every demonic principality. When you show up, demons flee. And when you show up, the atmosphere changes. Through your life, God desires that the lives of others are changed by the power of God. God desires that you are conscious that you are His ambassador and representative of His kingdom. You are a kingdom agent of transformation in Christ.

You were not created to blend in with darkness. Light has no relation with darkness. You were not created to blend in with the ways of satan's kingdom. You were created to shine with the glory of God. Satan's kingdom hates while God's kingdom loves. Satan's kingdom lives in unforgiveness and holds grudges while God's kingdom lives a life of forgiveness and forgives everyone who does them wrong. Satan's kingdom divides and God's Kingdom unites and lives in the peace of God. Satan's kingdom abides in sin while God's kingdom lives in the righteousness and holiness of God, in Christ Jesus. Satan's kingdom pursues a life of immorality and perversion while God's kingdom pursues purity and holiness in Christ Jesus. Satan's kingdom abides in evil and the appearance of evil, while God's kingdom completely avoids the appearance of evil. Satan's kingdom abides in darkness while God's kingdom abides in God's glorious light. Satan's kingdom is submerged in confusion while God's kingdom is submerged in the clarity of the Holy Spirit. We are submerged in supernatural peace that comes from God that supersedes human logic and human reasoning through a vibrant, personal relationship with God. Satan's kingdom is led and directed by demons. We, God's Kingdom, are led and directed by His Holy Spirit. Satan's kingdom is rooted in doubt and fear. We, God's kingdom, are rooted in faith, hope, and love that comes from the true living God of Abraham.

Step out and let the light of Christ shine in you, on you, and through you. Seek God's Kingdom first and His righteousness and watch everything be added to you according to His will and His glory. Live out of your personal relationship with God, live a life of repentance of sins, and faith in Jesus Christ. Run the race that God has called you to run with perseverance and endurance. Do not become lazy and fatigued doing what God has called you to do and being who He has called you to be. Do not be afraid to share your testimony with people, to pray for people, share the Gospel, and encourage people in Christ Jesus. Be bold and pray for the healing power of God to invade people's bodies and lives at the name of Jesus. Live in the fruits of the Holy Spirit out of your personal relationship with God. Live in the gifts of the Holy Spirit. Be the example, set the standard, be the role model in Christ Jesus, out of your relationship with Him.

Live out of your identity in Christ, from your authority in Him, and live out of the eternal victory in Christ. Jesus Christ defeated the devil with a score of one hundred to zero. He stripped him of all of his power. The only power the devil has is the power you give him through legal access or sin. Cast out demons at the name of Jesus Christ. Pray over your house, pray over your family, pray over your vehicle, pray before you leave your house. Plead the blood of Jesus Christ and declare the blood of Jesus. There is supernatural power in the blood of Jesus Christ. There is supernatural power in the name of Jesus Christ. Pray and worship God throughout the day. Declare the name of Jesus, speak words of faith, and speak the word of God. Bring people into the kingdom of God and live a life in Christ that draws lost, dying people into the kingdom of God, through repentance of sins and faith in Jesus Christ.

Declare the word of God over your life, over your family, situations, and circumstances. Be the change you want to see. Praise God instead of complaining, speak life instead of whining. In Christ Jesus, you are the solution to the world's confusion. In Christ Jesus, you have the answer to the world's problems and His Name is Jesus Christ of Nazareth. He is the Son of God, the King of Kings, the Lord of Lords, the Messiah, who rose from the dead victorious on the third day. JESUS conquered sin, death, the devil, his demons, and the grave. JESUS is the Holy Lamb of God who took away the sins of the world, who fulfilled all the old testament prophecies.

JESUS CHRIST is my Savior, He is my Lord, He is my protector. He is my refuge, strength, peace, and energy. He is my counselor, helper, everlasting life. He is my everything, my foundation. Jesus Christ is my rock, my new beginning, my identity, my empowerment, my authority, restoration, resurrection. He is my gifts, my skills, and my ability. He is my sanity, my joy, my healing, my clarity, my laughter, my gratitude, and my thankfulness. He is the reason I praise and worship God. He is my fulfillment, my overflow, and the beautiful, God-given, glorious, eternal list goes on.

The best decision you can make in this lifetime is repenting of your sins and putting your faith in Jesus Christ. The most important decision you will make is living for God and with everything you do, doing it unto Him for His glory, honor, and praise. The best decision you can make in your life is getting planted into a church that is centered on the Bible and on Jesus Christ. The best decision you can make in your lifetime is surrendering your heart to Jesus, choosing Him, and living one moment and day at a time with Him. Living for Him with radical gratitude and thankfulness unto the true living God is so important. You will never regret being kingdom of God-minded and body of Christ-minded. The best decision in your lifetime is building a relationship with JESUS and doing His work. There is nothing more exciting than building a relationship with JESUS and building His Kingdom through preaching, teaching, living, and demonstrating the Glorious Gospel of Jesus Christ.

The best decision you will make in this lifetime is allowing Him to live in you and through your life. You will never look back once you decide to receive everlasting life and bring heaven to earth through your personal relationship with God. After your heart stops you will transition to Heaven to be with God and His kingdom for eternity. The best decision you can make in this lifetime is to use the weaponry God gave you in Christ Jesus. Your weaponry is identifying with Jesus, using your authority in Christ, giving you continual victory over the defeated devil. Your weaponry is practicing living in the fruits of the Holy Spirit, the gifts of the Holy Spirit. Your weaponry is prayer, reading the Bible, worshiping God, speaking His word, and sharing the glorious gospel of Jesus Christ wherever you go. The best decision you can make in your lifetime is choosing Jesus Christ & living out of an ongoing, growing, life-giving living personal relationship with the true living God.

Confess this with me, "God, I ask you for the forgiveness of every sin I ever committed. Forgive me for opening doors for demonic activity through sin. I put my faith in your son, Jesus Christ. I confess with my mouth and believe with my heart that He is my Lord and Savior. I believe that He is your Son. I believe that He is The Messiah. I believe that He rose from the dead victorious on the third day. Jesus Christ, I receive your grace. I receive everything you made available through your life, bloodshed, resurrection, and ascension into Heaven at the right hand of God. Holy Spirit, I ask that you baptize me, fill me with your love, fire, and with your power. Holy Spirit, I ask you to fill me to overflow. God, I ask you to make my life a demonstration of your grace, love, and power. I cancel and break every demonic chain and stronghold that attached through decisions I have made, in the name of Jesus Christ. I command every demonic force and demonic entity to leave in the name of Jesus Christ. I dedicate my heart, my mind, my emotions, my body, my life, my house, everything I own to you, Jesus Christ. Holy Spirit, I give you complete access to every aspect of my life. From this day on, I will live for you with all of my heart, all of my thoughts, all of my emotions, all of my body, and all of my life, unto you, the true living God. My past, my present, and my future is bright because I have become one with Christ. Hallelujah in the mighty name of Jesus Christ, Amen."

Let These Bible Verses Encourage You

"Put on the whole armour of God, that ye may be able to stand against the wiles of the devil. For we wrestle not against flesh and blood, but against principalities, against powers, against the rulers of the darkness of this world, against spiritual wickedness in high places. Wherefore take unto you the whole armour of God, that ye may be able to withstand in the evil day, and having done all, to stand. Stand therefore, having your loins girt about with truth, and having on the breastplate of righteousness; and your feet shod with the preparation of the gospel of peace; above all, taking the shield of faith, wherewith ye shall be able to quench all the fiery darts of the wicked. And take the helmet of salvation, and the sword of the Spirit, which is the word of God: praying always with all prayer and supplication in the Spirit, and watching thereunto with all perseverance and supplication for all saints." Ephesians 6:11-18

"For the weapons of our warfare are not carnal, but mighty through God to the pulling down of strong holds;) casting down imaginations, and every high thing that exalteth itself against the knowledge of God, and bringing into captivity every thought to the obedience of Christ."
2 Corinthians 10:4-5

"And Jesus came and spake unto them, saying, All power is given unto me in heaven and in earth. Go ye therefore, and teach all nations, baptizing them in the name of the Father, and of the Son, and of the Holy Ghost: Teaching them to observe all things whatsoever I have commanded you: and, lo, I am with you always, even unto the end of the world. Amen." Matthew 28:18-20

"One day Jesus called together his twelve disciples and gave them power and authority to cast out all demons and to heal all diseases. Then he sent them out to tell everyone about the Kingdom of God and to heal the sick." Luke 9:1-2

"The Spirit of the Lord is upon me, because he hath anointed me to preach the gospel to the poor; he hath sent me to heal the brokenhearted, to preach deliverance to the captives, and

recovering of sight to the blind, to set at liberty them that are bruised, To preach the acceptable year of the Lord." Luke 4:18-19

"The thief cometh not, but for to steal, and to kill, and to destroy: I am come that they might have life, and that they might have it more abundantly." John 10:10

"That at the name of Jesus every knee should bow, of things in heaven, and things in earth, and things under the earth; And that every tongue should confess that Jesus Christ is Lord, to the glory of God the Father. Wherefore, my beloved, as ye have always obeyed, not as in my presence only, but now much more in my absence, work out your own salvation with fear and trembling." Philippians 2:10-12

"Neither is there salvation in any other: for there is none other name under heaven given among men, whereby we must be saved." Acts 4:12

"And he said unto them, Go ye into all the world, and preach the gospel to every creature. He that believeth and is baptized shall be saved; but he that believeth not shall be damned. And these signs shall follow them that believe; In my name shall they cast out devils; they shall speak with new tongues; They shall take up serpents; and if they drink any deadly thing, it shall not hurt them; they shall lay hands on the sick, and they shall recover. So then after the Lord had spoken unto them, he was received up into heaven, and sat on the right hand of God. And they went forth, and preached every where, the Lord working with them, and confirming the word with signs following. Amen." Mark 16:15-20

Chapter 17

THE POWER OF FORGIVENESS

Unforgiveness is dangerous. When someone holds onto grudges and bitterness and chooses not to forgive, they put themselves in a place where a door is legally open for demonic torment. Unforgiveness is like drinking poison and hoping the other person is affected by the poison. Unforgiveness does not make the other person feel heavy and weighed down. It only makes *you* feel heavy and weighed down. You do not have to wait for the feeling to forgive before you choose to forgive. If you are holding onto unforgiveness, you can forgive the person or situation that hurt you by faith. You can release what hurt and offended you to God by faith.

When you sow the seed of forgiveness, you give God an open door to invade the entire situation with His grace and love. Just because you forgive the person does not mean you give them access to you. Every situation is different so allow the Holy Spirit to guide and direct. There are certain people you have to show "Agape love" to from a distance and that is ok. Agape love is God's love flowing through you. Forgiveness frees you from the heavyweight and prison of bitterness. Forgiveness liberates you from the "straitjacket" of offense.

You get your empowerment to forgive out of a revelation of how much God loves you, proven through Jesus Christ. You receive empowerment to forgive out of a revelation of the forgiveness that was made available to you through Jesus Christ. You receive the gasoline needed to forgive out of your personal relationship with God. We did not deserve forgiveness, yet Jesus Christ still made it available and paid the price for it before we were ever born. God loves us, His creation, so much that He still made forgiveness available to humanity even though we did not deserve it.

If You Are Holding On To Unforgiveness In Your Heart...

The first step is to by faith ask God for forgiveness for holding onto the sin of unforgiveness. Say a prayer of repentance and faith in Jesus Christ. Declare, "Jesus, I ask you for mercy, I ask for forgiveness of my sins, all of my faith is in you." The second thing you need to do is by faith, open up your mouth and say, "Thank you for your love for me my God, thank you for your mercy, thank you for your grace that you have shown me." Then declare by faith, "I forgive every single person that hurt me in the past." Then say, "God forgive me for every single person that I might have hurt in the past." The third step is to declare by faith, "Soak me in your tangible love, God. Make me a demonstration of your Agape love." Take a deep breath in and declare by faith, "Holy Spirit, I ask you to fill me afresh, in Jesus' Name."

As you sow the seed of forgiveness, you open up yourself to experience God's grace in your life in ways you never thought or imagined. Love God... Love people… Live a life of forgiveness. You are loved! Living a life of agape love and forgiveness is a refreshing place to be. Remember we are the hands and feet of Jesus, a tangible expression of God's heart on the earth

Unity

One of the number one things that the devil hates is unity. He does not want you to have unity with Jesus, your family, friends, or the body of Christ. The devil wants division and God desires us to live in unity.

God desires that every disciple of Jesus lives in the fruits of the Holy Spirit. We do this by seeking His kingdom first and His righteousness, out of identity in Christ and from the position of relationship. As we center our lives on the kingdom of God through prayer, reading the Bible, worshiping Him, declaring His word, and manifesting the love of Christ to the earth in some kind of way, we center our lives on His Kingdom. By communing with Him and living out of a relationship with Him, the fruits of the Spirit will freely spring out of you. Galatians 5:22-23 says, "But the fruit of the Spirit is love, joy, peace, forbearance, kindness, goodness, faithfulness, gentleness and self-control."

God desires that we live in unity with Him and that we reflect His love, light, and glory to the earth. We were never meant to blend in with the ways of the world. We were created to stand out and to shine bright through the ways of God. The world hates but God desires that we love. The world gets offended and holds grudges but God desires that we forgive quickly. The world's mouth is filled with negativity and filth. God desires that love, light, and truth comes out of our mouths. The world lives according to the flesh but God created us to live according to His Spirit. The world is rude but God desires that we live in kindness.

Jesus Christ is the light and hope of this world. As born-again believers, He is living on the inside of us. This means that through Him we are the hope and light of the world. The world is growing darker, which means we should be shining *brighter*. Let your light shine. Be the change. Be the difference. Be the solution. Allow the glory and light of Heaven to shine in you, on you, and through you, in Christ Jesus.

Let These Bible Verses Encourage You

"Then said Jesus, Father, forgive them; for they know not what they do. And they parted his raiment, and cast lots."
Luke 23:34

"And he kneeled down, and cried with a loud voice, Lord, lay not this sin to their charge. And when he had said this, he fell asleep." Acts 7:60

"Blessed are the merciful: for they shall obtain mercy."
Matthew 5:7

"But if ye forgive not men their trespasses, neither will your Father forgive your trespasses." Mathew 6:15

*"Let all bitterness, and wrath, and anger, and clamour, and evil speaking, be put away from you, with all malice: "And be ye kind one to another, tenderhearted, forgiving one another, even as God for Christ's sake hath forgiven you."
Ephesians 4:31-32*

"And whenever you stand praying, forgive, if you have anything against anyone, so that your Father also who is in heaven may forgive you your trespasses." Mark 11:25

"Forbearing one another, and forgiving one another, if any man have a quarrel against any: even as Christ forgave you, so also do ye." Colossians 3:13

*"And forgive us our debts, as we forgive our debtors."
Matthew 6:12*

*"If we confess our sins, he is faithful and just to forgive us our sins, and to cleanse us from all unrighteousness."
1 John 1:9*

*"He hath not dealt with us after our sins; Nor rewarded us according to our iniquities. For as the heaven is high above the earth, So great is his mercy toward them that fear him. As far as the east is from the west, So far hath he removed our transgressions from us. Like as a father pitieth his children, So the LORD pitieth them that fear him. For he knoweth our frame; He remembereth that we are dust."
Psalm 103:10-14*

*"For I will be merciful to their unrighteousness, and their sins and their iniquities will I remember no more."
Hebrews 8:12*

"But God demonstrated his love toward us, in that, while we were yet sinners, Christ died for us." Romans 5:8

"This is a faithful saying, and worthy of all acceptance, that Christ Jesus came into the world to save sinners; of whom I am chief. Howbeit for this cause I obtained mercy, that in me first Jesus Christ might shew forth all longsuffering, for a pattern to them which should hereafter believe on him to life everlasting." 1 Timothy 1:15-16

"Then said Jesus, Father, forgive them; for they know not what they do. And they parted his raiment, and cast lots." Luke 23:34

"Do all that you can to live in peace with everyone. Dear friends, never take revenge. Leave that to the righteous anger of God. For the Scriptures say, I will take revenge; I will pay them back, says the LORD. Instead, If your enemies are hungry, feed them. If they are thirsty, give them something to drink. In doing this, you will heap burning coals of shame on their heads. Don't let evil conquer you, but conquer evil by doing good." Romans 12:18-21

"But I tell you not to resist an evil person. But whoever slaps you on your right cheek, turn the other to him also. If anyone wants to sue you and take away your tunic, let him have your cloak also. And whoever compels you to go one mile, go with him two." Matthew 5:39-41

"He who covers a transgression seeks love, But he who repeats a matter separates friends." Proverbs 17:9

"But love your enemies, do good to them, and lend to them without expecting to get anything back. Then your reward will be great, and you will be children of the Most High, because he is kind to the ungrateful and wicked. Be merciful, just as your Father is merciful." Luke 6:35-36

"Hatred stirreth up strifes: But love covereth all sins." Proverbs 10:12

"For God so loved the world, that he gave his only begotten Son, that whosoever believeth in him should not perish, but have everlasting life. For God sent not his Son into the world to condemn the world; but that the world through him might be saved." John 3:16-17

"But the fruit of the Spirit is love, joy, peace, longsuffering, gentleness, goodness, faith, Meekness, temperance: against such there is no law." Galatians 5:22

"Then Peter came to Him and said, 'Lord, how often shall my brother sin against me, and I forgive him? Up to seven times?' Jesus said to him, 'I do not say to you, up to seven times, but up to seventy times seven.' Therefore the kingdom of heaven is like a certain king who wanted to settle accounts with his servants. And when he had begun to settle accounts, one was brought to him who owed him ten thousand talents. But as he was not able to pay, his master commanded that he be sold, with his wife and children and all that he had, and that payment be made. The servant therefore fell down before him, saying, 'Master, have patience with me, and I will pay you all.' Then the master of that servant was moved with compassion, released him, and forgave him the debt. But that servant went out and found one of his fellow servants who owed him a hundred denarii; and he laid hands on him and took him by the throat, saying, 'Pay me what you owe!' So his fellow servant fell down at his feet and begged him, saying, 'Have patience with me, and I will pay you all.' And he would not, but went and threw him into prison till he should pay the debt. So when his fellow servants saw what had been done, they were very grieved, and came and told their master all that had been done. Then his master, after he had called him, said to him, 'You wicked servant! I forgave you all that debt because you begged me. Should you not also have had compassion on your fellow servant, just as I had pity on you?' And his master was angry, and delivered him to the torturers until he should pay all that was due to him. 'So My heavenly Father also will do

to you if each of you, from his heart, does not forgive his brother his trespasses.'" Matthew 18:21-35

CHAPTER 18
THE POWER OF TIME MANAGEMENT

God desires that we manage our time with excellence and integrity. God has given us a twenty-four hour circulation called a "day" to know Him and to make Him known. He has given us this time to accomplish what He has called us to do. He desires that we are productive and produce with what He has given us. The secret to our God-given futures is hidden in our God-given, daily routine. What gets accomplished in a day is done by someone utilizing their time correctly. What we do with our time determines what gets accomplished. Some people complain about not having jobs but when you ask them if they have filled out job applications, most of the time they say "no." Of course, this is not always the case. But if they would take time to fill out applications, pray over those applications, and believe God for a job, the right job would contact them and they would get hired.

There is power in managing our God-given time correctly. When we manage our time the way God desires us to manage it, God is glorified. God does not want us to waste time or "throw it away." The Bible says that God desires for us to "be fruitful and multiply." As we work with what He has given us, He will cause it to grow and multiply it.

God desires that we utilize the calendar, create schedules, organize and categorize our goals. He wants us to have our priorities in order, according to the Bible. Things do not just happen by chance; oftentimes things happen because actions took place. Think about the law of sowing seed. We first plant the seeds, then water them. Seeds then receive sunlight, and when planted in the right atmosphere and nurtured, the seed eventually grows into a tree. It turns into a fruitful tree as long as it is in the right environment. As long as it is catered to correctly, with sunlight and water, it will grow.

It works the same way with different God-given goals that we have. For example, if someone wants to get fit, healthy, or gain muscle mass, they must work out right, eat and hydrate correctly, and get adequate sleep. Under those circumstances, their muscles will grow, and they will get fit and healthy. You do not need to *hope* you will gain muscle mass and that you will get fit when you are doing all the right things. In the same way, when you plant the right seeds, water them correctly, and put them in the right atmosphere, the results happen freely. You can apply this law of the seed to anything in your life.

God created the law of seedtime and harvest. Plant the seed, water the seed, nurture the seed, give it sunlight, put it in the right atmosphere, and it will grow, every single time. If you apply the law of the seed to your life, you will produce the fruit that you desire to see. Allow God's Holy Spirit to guide you in all things. Choose to produce with what God has given you and avoid wasting the time that God has given you by seeking Him first, yielding to His voice, and advancing His kingdom. God is glorified when we do so! God does not desire that we waste our time. He desires that we invest our time into His kingdom and that we produce with what He has put into our hands.

I pray that the wisdom, knowledge, and understanding of the Holy Spirit invades your life. I Pray that He would give you the wisdom on how to organize your time. I believe He will give you the wisdom to create schedules for your God-given priorities. I pray that God will direct you in all that you do in the mighty name of JESUS!

The law of seedtime and harvest can be applied to anything and everything. Be alert with the seeds that you plant, water, and nurture. The seeds that you plant, water, and nurture determine the kind of fruits that you harvest. Allow the Holy Spirit to reveal to you what seeds you should be planting, watering, and nurturing. Allow the Holy Spirit to show you what seeds you need to stop planting, stop watering, and stop nurturing. The thoughts you think, the words you speak, and the things that you do are either seeds, water that you are pouring onto the seeds, or sunlight. After a while, whether you realize it or not, you will reap a harvest. Whether it is a good harvest or a bad harvest, simply depends on the kind of seeds that you are planting, watering, and nurturing. If you do not like the harvest that you are reaping, simply change the seeds that you are planting, watering, and nurturing. Once again, be alert on what you plant, water, and nurture. Everything that you plant, water, and nurture will grow. Make sure that what you plant, water, and nurture lines up with the word of God, and His destiny for your life. Be sure that it is in line with what He is telling you to do. Remember, God knows and wants what is best for you. He desires that you trust him and obey Him so you can experience His best for you.

Let These Bible Verses Encourage You

"See then that ye walk circumspectly, not as fools, but as wise, redeeming the time, because the days are evil. Wherefore be ye not unwise, but understanding what the will of the Lord is." Ephesians 5:15-17

"Behave wisely toward outsiders, making the best use of your time." Colossians 4:5

Seek wisdom from the Lord...

"So teach us to number our days, That we may apply our hearts unto wisdom." Psalm 90:12

"If any of you lack wisdom, let him ask of God, that giveth to all men liberally, and upbraideth not; and it shall be given him." James 1:5

Live eternity-minded...

"While we look not at the things which are seen, but at the things which are not seen: for the things which are seen are temporal; but the things which are not seen are eternal."
2 Corinthians 4:18

"He hath made every thing beautiful in his time: also he hath set the world in their heart, so that no man can find out the work that God maketh from the beginning to the end."
Ecclesiastes 3:11

"Therefore we are always confident and know that as long as we are at home in the body we are away from the Lord. For we live by faith, not by sight. We are confident, I say, and would prefer to be away from the body and at home with the Lord. So we make it our goal to please him, whether we are at home in the body or away from it. For we must all appear before the judgment seat of Christ, so that each of us may receive what is due us for the things done while in the body, whether good or bad."
2 Corinthians 5:6-10

Live in the moment, live in the now, be fully alive in the present...

"Do not boast about tomorrow, For you do not know what a day may bring forth."
Proverbs 27:1

"Come now, you who say, "Today or tomorrow we will go to such and such a city, spend a year there, buy and sell, and make a profit"; whereas you do not know what will happen tomorrow. For what is your life? It is even a vapor that appears for a little time and then vanishes away."
James 4:13-14

Do not procrastinate! Make plans for the future...

"For which of you, wanting to build a tower, doesn't first sit down and calculate the cost to see if he has enough to complete it?"
Luke 14:28

"The plans of the diligent lead only to plenty, but everyone who is hasty comes only to poverty."
Proverbs 21:5

Consider the ant, you lazy bum. Watch its ways, and become wise. Although it has no overseer, officer, or ruler, in summertime it stores its food supply. At harvest time it gathers its food.
Proverbs 6:6-8

Allow the Holy Spirit to guide you in all things...

"A person plans his way, but the LORD directs his steps."
Proverbs 16:9

"But when he, the Spirit of truth, comes, he will guide you into all truth. For he will not speak on his own authority, but will speak whatever he hears, and will tell you what is to come."
John 16:13

Create time for God every day...

"As for me, I will call upon God; And the LORD shall save me. Evening, and morning, and at noon, will I pray, and cry aloud: And he shall hear my voice."
Psalm 55:16-17

Prioritize, organize, and set goals...

"Moses' father-in-law replied, "What you are doing is not good. You and these people who come to you will only wear yourselves out. The work is too heavy for you; you cannot

handle it alone. Listen now to me and I will give you some advice, and may God be with you. You must be the people's representative before God and bring their disputes to him. Teach them his decrees and instructions, and show them the way they are to live and how they are to behave. But select capable men from all the people—men who fear God, trustworthy men who hate dishonest gain—and appoint them as officials over thousands, hundreds, fifties and tens."
Exodus 18:17-21

"But seek ye first his kingdom, and his righteousness; and all these things shall be added unto you."
Matthew 6:33

Put all of your trust in the Lord...

"But I trusted in thee, O LORD: I said, Thou art my God. My times are in thy hand: Deliver me from the hand of mine enemies, and from them that persecute me." Psalm 31:14-15

"Commit your way to the Lord, Trust also in Him, And He shall bring it to pass."
Psalm 37:5

Good work ethic is key...

"In all labor there is profit, But idle chatter leads only to poverty."
Proverbs 14:23

"Do not love sleep, lest you come to poverty; Open your eyes, and you will be satisfied with bread."
Proverbs 20:13

"How long will you lie there, you sluggard? When will you get up from your sleep? A little sleep, a little slumber, a little folding of the hands to rest— and poverty will come on you like a thief and scarcity like an armed man."
Proverbs 6:9-11

"He becometh poor that dealeth with a slack hand: But the hand of the diligent maketh rich."
Proverbs 10:4

Keep running the race of Faith...

"Fight the good fight of faith, lay hold on eternal life, whereunto thou art also called, and hast professed a good profession before many witnesses."
1 Timothy 6:12

"To everything there is a season, A time for every purpose under heaven: A time to be born, And a time to die; A time to plant, And a time to pluck what is planted."
Ecclesiastes 3:1-2

"Do you not know that those who run in a race all run, but only one receives the prize? Run in such a way that you may win."
1 Corinthians 9:24

"Therefore we also, since we are surrounded by so great a cloud of witnesses, let us lay aside every weight, and the sin which so easily ensnares us, and let us run with endurance the race that is set before us, looking unto Jesus, the author and finisher of our faith, who for the joy that was set before Him endured the cross, despising the shame, and has sat down at the right hand of the throne of God."
Hebrews 12:1-2

CHAPTER 19

LOOK WHAT THE LORD HAS DONE

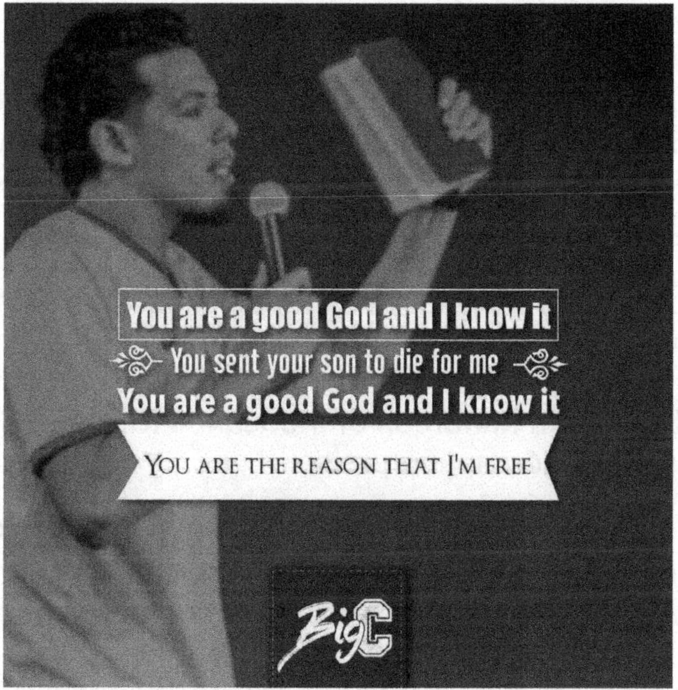

I wrote this book to give God praise, honor, and glory. His grace has allowed me to start Saving Our Generation Ministries as a foundation to reach the nations with the glorious Gospel of Jesus Christ. His grace has empowered and allowed me to release Jesus Christ-filled, kingdom of God rooted music albums and music videos in different languages. His grace has allowed me to travel across the United States, ministering the glorious, saving message of Jesus

Christ. His grace has allowed me to travel to Brazil twenty-five times and minister in thirty two cities, and the numbers are still growing. His grace has allowed me to minister in different nations of the world. He has allowed me to host gospel concerts, crusades, festivals, tent revivals, and minister in prisons. He opened the door for me to be on national and international television and the radio. God's grace has allowed me to launch a weekly Saturday JESUS gathering called "Grand Finale Jesus Movement Revival" in Tulsa Oklahoma, where people are getting saved, healed, and set free every single week through the glorious gospel of Jesus Christ. By His grace alone I have been able to share the good news of Jesus in supermarkets, malls, gas stations, and in the streets. He opened the door for me to speak in school assemblies nationally and internationally. By the grace of God, He has allowed me to minister to over a million people and win hundreds of thousands to Jesus Christ for His glory, honor, and praise.

We serve a God of miracles who can take what seems like nothing and turn it into something. He can take what the world sees as "trash" and turn it into a diamond. God is love, God loves you, He loves me, and Jesus Christ proved it through His life, bloodshed, death, and resurrection. I know that greater things are ahead in the mighty Name of JESUS! I praise God for the past, present, and future. I look forward to hosting more evangelistic events, reaching more souls for JESUS, releasing more albums, music videos, and books. I am excited to work on and execute more God-given projects, all to glorify God and grow His Kingdom by channeling the gospel of Jesus Christ through different avenues.

Before I surrendered my heart to Jesus, I did not value school and got kicked out of different schools for bad behavior. But God transformed life and made me a brand new person, as you have read in my book. My life was going in the wrong direction and things were not looking good until I surrendered my heart to Jesus Christ in 2007. After God's power intervened in my life that year, through my first trip to Heaven, His grace allowed me to get a Bible college degree from Rhema Bible Training College and a Bachelor's degree for His glory from Oral Roberts University. Those were true miracles of God. It is amazing what God does when we say "yes" to JESUS. It is amazing what God does when we are faithful to His voice. What a joy it is to know Him, build a relationship with him, and make Him known.

Be encouraged by the God-given visions, dreams, out-of-body experiences, and teaching chapters in this book. Be encouraged by the Biblical teaching in this book. This book is a kingdom resource that will help lay a Biblical foundation for your Christian walk. Let it inspire you and motivate you to be who God has called you to be. I believe as you read it over and over it will bless you in different ways. Let it encourage you to step out and do what God has called you to do. No matter what He calls you to do, this book is a tool for God's glory, power, and love to flow in you, on you, and through you.

There is God-given purpose all over your life. There is a God-given purpose behind why you are holding this book in your hand. This is not a normal book and God knew that you were going to read it. I did not want to serve God, be in ministry, or live for Jesus. I had other plans, I had other goals, I had other desires. I could not outrun the love and grace of God. It chased me down until the only thing I could do was surrender to it. I had people praying for me, my parents and other believers. Those prayers caused God to reach out to me in a supernatural way when I was eighteen years old, as you read in earlier chapters. There is power in prayer and we serve a God of miracles. I am a miracle and my miraculous story is still being written. You are a miracle and your miraculous story is still being written.

Once again, reading this book will help you lay a biblical foundation. Out of this foundation, I believe God is going to use your life to eternally impact this world for Jesus Christ. Let this book fuel you to live a life of faith in the Lord Jesus Christ. Let it fuel your faith so you can live with a revelation of the eternal hope in Jesus Christ and the grace of God that has been poured out on your life. Let it fuel your faith to live with a revelation of the love of God. Allow the Holy Spirit to guide you and direct you in all things.

Allow this book to stir up a conviction from the Holy Spirit that propels you forward in the calling that God has on your life. Let it launch you into living a life that glorifies Him from a place of freedom and liberty. Let it encourage you to live from a place of joyful empowerment from the Holy Spirit of God. The Christian life was never meant to be lived out of your own ability. It was meant to be lived from His ability, His strength, and His empowerment. You cannot live the Christian life without Christ. It is only lived out of a vibrant, living, and growing personal relationship with Him.

Let this book encourage you to live your life rooted in the love of God, where you see people through the lens of God's love and where He flows through you from His love. Let it help you to fulfill the call of God on your life. As the body of Christ, our motive is the love of God. As the body of Christ, our "why" is the love of God. As the body of Christ, our gasoline and fuel is the love of God for us, proven through the life, bloodshed, death, and resurrection of the Lord Jesus Christ. Praise God for His supernatural love.

Allow God's love proven through Jesus Christ to compel you to repent of your sins, turn away from your sins, and put your faith in Jesus Christ as your Lord Savior. Believe that God raised Him from the dead, knowing that Jesus Christ lived for you, died for you, and shed His blood for you. Every drop of blood that was shed from the body of Jesus yelled out, "I love you." He died, shed His blood for you, and rose from the dead for you, so that you could be forgiven of your sins and washed completely clean. Dirty blood cannot wash you clean but the perfect, righteous, Holy blood of Jesus Christ that was shed for you can wash you clean.

By repenting and putting faith in Jesus Christ as your Lord and savior, surrendering your heart, mind, emotions, thoughts, words, body, and life to Him, you became clean. Remember you are as innocent as the blood that you have been washed in. If you have been washed in the blood of Jesus Christ, you are forgiven and innocent. Jesus Christ came for you so you could become a Child of God, a brand new creation in Him, so you can be born again, born of Him, born of His love, born into His Family, and engrafted into His victorious kingdom. He laid down His life so that you could have a transforming, fulfilling, personal relationship with Him.

Thank you for reading my God-given book, *Do Not Be Afraid, Heaven is Real*. I want to remind you that your life is valuable. Your life is precious, you matter, and you are important. Once again, you have God's purpose all over your life. The true living God, our Heavenly Father, is a God of forgiveness, love, and mercy. His arms are wide open and ready to receive you. He is ready to embrace you. He loves you. I pray that this God-given piece of literature has been and is a blessing to you. I believe in you, I love you, and know that God is going to use your life as an instrument of His Grace. To God be all of the honor, glory, and praise, in Jesus Christ's Name, Amen.

Praise God for the past, present, and future! *In Christ Jesus, the past is bright because the blood of Jesus turned our past into a testimony. In Christ Jesus, the present is bright because our identity is in Christ Jesus and the glory and presence of God abide within us. In Christ Jesus, the* *future is bright because the true living God, our Glorious Heavenly Father, holds our future in His hands.* **In Christ Jesus the past, present, and future is bright!**

*Remember we are the **hands** and **feet** of **JESUS**, a **tangible expression** of **GOD's heart** on the **earth**.*

What exciting days we are living in, to be ALIVE IN CHRIST JESUS! JESUS CHRIST IS COMING SOON... Until He does, let us continue to invade our hurting cities with the glorious, healing, saving message of the great news of Jesus Christ! HALLELUJAH TO MOST HIGH GOD!

YOUR
BEST DAYS
ARE RIGHT
IN FRONT
OF YOU

SALVATION PRAYER OF REPENTANCE, FAITH & COMMITMENT

Confess this with me: *"God, I ask you for the forgiveness of every sin I ever committed. Forgive me for opening doors for demonic activity through sin. I put my faith in your son Jesus Christ, I confess with my mouth and believe with my heart that He is my Lord and Savior. I believe that He is your son, I believe that He is the Messiah, I believe that He rose from the dead victorious on the third day. Jesus Christ, I receive your grace. I receive everything you made available through your life, bloodshed, resurrection, and ascension into Heaven, at the right hand of God. Holy Spirit, I ask that you baptize me, fill me with your love, fire, and with your power. Holy Spirit, I ask you to fill me to overflow. God, I ask you to make my life a demonstration of your grace, love, and power. I cancel and break every demonic chain and stronghold that attached through decisions I have made in the past, in the name of Jesus Christ. I command every demonic force and demonic entity to leave in the name of Jesus Christ. I dedicate my heart, my mind, my emotions, my body, my life, my house, everything I own to you, Jesus Christ. Holy Spirit, I give you complete access to every aspect of my life. From this day on, I will live for you with all of my heart, all of my thoughts, all of my emotions, all of my body, and all of my life, unto you true living God. My past, my present, and my future is bright because I have become one with you, Christ. Hallelujah in the mighty name of Jesus Christ, Amen."*

SIGN____

DATE____

TEAR OUT AND MAIL TO: Saving Our Generation Ministries-P.O. Box 702624 Tulsa, OK, 74170
We praise God and celebrate your decision to begin a personal relationship with JESUS. Welcome to the family of God! We are praying for you! Your best days are right in front of you! God is going to use your life to eternally impact this world through the gospel of Jesus Christ!

BE ENCOURAGED

Who are you...

You are a child of God and a joint heir with Jesus Christ. (Rom. 8:16-17). You are a temple of the Holy Spirit. (1st Cor 6:18-20). You can come before God at any time in prayer. (Eph. 2:18). You can be confident that God hears your prayers. (1 John 5:14-15) You can approach God with boldness and confidence. (Ephesians 3:12).

You can be greatly blessed by being persistent in prayers. (Luke 11:5-13, 18:1-8). You can pray for more faith for it brings more blessings. (Mark 9:24, Luke 17:5-6). You can praise God for He works wonders when He is praised (Exodus 5:11). You can pray the Lord's prayer as it was given to you by Jesus Christ, when you come to the end keep praying (Matt 6:9-13).

You are protected...

You are born of God and the wicked one cannot touch you (1 John 5:18). You can obtain mercy and grace to help in a time of need (Hebrews 4:16). You are protected by God (Psalms 91, 103:3). You are in Christ Jesus and free from condemnation (Romans 8:1). You will dwell in the house of the Lord forever (Psalms 23:6). You are a friend of Jesus Christ and appointed to bear fruit (John 15:14-17). You can gain strength and protection by memorizing God's Word (Hebrews 4:12). You are secure in Christ and cannot be separated from God (Romans 8:31-39). You have been given power, love, a sound mind and freedom from fear (2 Timothy 1:7).

You are special...

You are the salt and light of the world (Matthew 5:13-16). You are established, anointed and sealed by God (2nd Cor 1:21-22). You are fearfully and wonderfully made (Psalms 139:14). You have God's peace that surpasses all understanding (Philippians 4:6-9). You can overcome the world with faith in Jesus Christ (1 John 5:4-5). You are to communicate God's word to all people (Mark 16:15). You can do all things through Jesus Christ who strengthens you (Philipians 4:13). You will be able to escape and endure temptation (1 Corinthians 10:13). You are a new creature in Christ Jesus: the old things have passed away, behold all things have become new (2 Corinthians 5:17).

God knows you...
But the very hairs of your head are all numbered (Matthew 10:30).

God loves you...
For God so loved the world, that he gave his only begotten Son, that whosoever believeth in him should not perish, but have everlasting life (John 3:16). If we confess our sins, he is faithful and just to forgive us our sins, and to cleanse us from all unrighteousness (John 1:9).

Sin separates you from God...
As it is written, There is none righteous, no, not one: Romans 3:10. For all have sinned, and come short of the glory of God (Romans 3:23).

God's remedy for all sin...
Christ died for our sins according to the Scriptures; and that he was buried, and that he rose again, the third day according to the scriptures 1 Corinthians 15:3-5. For the wages of sin is death; but the gift of God is eternal life through Jesus Christ our Lord (Romans 6:23). Jesus saith unto him, I am the way, the truth, and the life: no man cometh unto the Father, but by me (John 14:6).

All can be saved...
For whosoever shall call upon the name of the Lord shall be saved (Romans 10:13).

God's gift of eternal life...
That if thou shalt confess with thy mouth the Lord Jesus, and shalt believe in thine heart that God hath raised him from the dead, thou shalt be saved (Romans 10:9).
For by grace are ye saved through faith; and that not of yourselves: it is the gift of God (Ephesians 2:8-9).

TO CONTACT BOOK OR CONNECT

Saving Our Generation Ministries
P.O. Box 702624 Tulsa, Oklahoma, 74170
918-504-6527
BookBigCNow@gmail.com
SOGGlobal.Org
GrandFinaleJesusMovement.com
ChrisBigCSlager.com
Instagram.com/BigC777
facebook.com/BigC777
Twitter.com/BigC777
Youtube.com/MisterBigC777

MORE RESOURCES FROM CHRISTOPHER SLAGER "BIG C"

Music Projects

Grand Finale Album

Grand Finale 2 Album

Grand Finale 3 Album

Heroic Album

A Gift To The World Mixtape

Electricity Album

Jesus Christ Is Lord Album

JESUS É O ÚNICO QUE SALVA Album

Grand Finale Jesus Movement Album

Hallelujah Album

Music Videos

God Did Not Give Me A Spirit Of Fear - Big C

I'm Here To Make History - Big C

Addicted To His Love - Big C

Dança Igual David- Big C

Nada Vai Me Parar - Big C

Fala Não Pra Tentação - Big C

Eu Sou Amado Por Deus - Big C

Tudo E Possível - Big C

Deus Está Comigo - Big C

Books

Do Not Be Afraid Heaven Is Real

@BigC777

THE GOSPEL SOUL-WINNING
—SCRIPT—

Has anyone ever told you that God loves you and that He has a wonderful plan for your life? I have a real quick, but important question to ask you. If you were to die this very second, do you know for sure, beyond a shadow of a doubt, that you would go to Heaven? [If "Yes"—Great, why would you say "Yes"? (If they respond with anything but "I have Jesus in my heart" or something similar to that, PROCEED WITH SCRIPT) or "No" or "I hope so" PROCEED WITH SCRIPT.]

Let me quickly share with you what the Holy Bible reads. It reads "for all have sinned and come short of the glory of God" and "for the wages of sin is death, but the gift of God is eternal life through Jesus Christ our Lord". The Bible also reads, "For whosoever shall call upon the name of the Lord shall be saved". And you're a "whosoever" right? Of course you are; all of us are.

I'm going to say a quick prayer for you. Lord, bless (FILL IN NAME) and his/her family with long and healthy lives. Jesus, make Yourself real to him/her and do a quick work in his/her heart. If (FILL IN NAME) has not received Jesus Christ as his/her Lord and Savior, I pray he/she will do so now.

(FILL IN NAME), if you would like to receive the gift that God has for you today, say this after me with your heart and lips out loud. Dear Lord Jesus, come into my heart. Forgive me of my sin. Wash me and cleanse me. Set me free. Jesus, thank You that You died for me. I believe that You are risen from the dead and that You're coming back again for me. Fill me with the Holy Spirit. Give me a passion for the lost, a hunger for the things of God and a holy boldness to preach the gospel of Jesus Christ. I'm saved; I'm born again, I'm forgiven and I'm on my way to Heaven because I have Jesus in my heart.

As a minister of the gospel of Jesus Christ, I tell you today that all of your sins are forgiven. Always remember to run to God and not from God because He loves you and has a great plan for your life.

[Invite them to your church and get follow up info: name, address, & phone number.]

NOTES

Made in the USA
Coppell, TX
20 September 2024